Space and Language in Architectural Education

Architects habitually disregard disciplinary boundaries of their profession in search for synergies and inspiration. The realm of language, although not considered to be architects' natural environment, opens opportunities to further stretch and expand the architectural imagination and the set of tools used in the design process. When used in the context of architectural pedagogy, the exploration of the relationship between space and language opens the discussion further to include the reflection on the design studio structure, the learning process in creative subjects, and the ethical dimension of architectural education.

This book offers a glimpse into architectural pedagogies exploring the relationship between space and language, using literary methods and linguistic experiments. The examples discuss a wide range of approaches from international perspective, exploring opportunities and challenges of engaging literary methods and linguistic experiments in architectural education.

The theme of *Catalysts* discusses the use of literary methods in architectural pedagogy, where literary texts are used to jump-start and support the design process, resulting in deeply contextual approaches capable of subverting embedded hierarchies of the design studio. *Tensions* explore the gap between the world and its description, employing linguistic experiments and literary methods to enrich and expand the architectural vocabulary to include the experience of space in its infinite complexity.

This book will be useful for innovators in architectural education and those seeking to expand their teaching practice to incorporate literary methods, and to creatives interested in making teaching a part of their practice. It may also appeal to students from design-based disciplines with an established design studio culture, demonstrating how to use narrative, poetry, and literature to expand and feed your imagination.

Kasia Nawratek is a senior lecturer at Manchester School of Architecture, United Kingdom, a qualified architect and a writer. Her current research interests focus on the climate crisis response in architectural education using post-human perspectives, and literary methods in studio-based pedagogical methodologies. Her teaching practice is underpinned by Mikhail Bakhtin's idea of polyphony which fosters an inclusive and dialogic studio culture.

Routledge Focus on Design Pedagogy
Series Editor: Graham Cairns

The Routledge Focus on Design Pedagogy series provides the reader with the latest scholarship for instructors who educate designers. The series publishes research from across the globe and covers areas as diverse as beginning design and foundational design, architecture, product design, interior design, fashion design, landscape architecture, urban design, and architectural conservation and historic preservation. By making these studies available to the world-wide academic community, the series aims to promote quality design education.

Fluid Space and Transformational Learning
Kyriaki Tsoukala

Progressive Studio Pedagogy
Examples from Architecture and Allied Design Fields
Edited by Charlie Smith

Emerging Practices in Architectural Pedagogy
Accommodating an Uncertain Future
Edited by Laura Sanderson and Sally Stone

For more information about this series, please visit: https://www.routledge.com/architecture/series/RFDP

Space and Language in Architectural Education
Catalysts and Tensions

Edited by
Kasia Nawratek

Routledge
Taylor & Francis Group

LONDON AND NEW YORK

First published 2022
by Routledge
4 Park Square, Milton Park, Abingdon, Oxon OX14 4RN

and by Routledge
605 Third Avenue, New York, NY 10158

Routledge is an imprint of the Taylor & Francis Group, an informa business

British Library Cataloguing-in-Publication Data
A catalogue record for this book is available from the British Library

Library of Congress Cataloging-in-Publication Data
A catalog record has been requested for this book

ISBN: 978-1-032-19382-3 (hbk)
ISBN: 978-1-032-19384-7 (pbk)
ISBN: 978-1-003-25893-3 (ebk)

DOI: 10.4324/9781003258933

Typeset in Times NR MT Pro
by KnowledgeWorks Global Ltd.

Contents

Introduction

Kasia Nawratek

Open a book, flip through the opening pages, arrive on the Introduction page. Here you are, following marks on paper or a screen with your eyes, your brain firing up connections to conjure an image of yourself, reading. Now you see yourself in a mirror of your mind. A connection is formed, as I type these words on a train moving through the misty Hope Valley between Sheffield and Manchester and I am thinking of you, the reader. In just a few sentences, two images appeared: of yourself, the reader, and a train moving through the mist, with the author onboard, typing. We are in different spaces and timelines, yet connected.

Literary imagination, this would be a useful term to use here. The seemingly magic trick our minds play on us when we encounter language. Assemblages of words trigger connections in our brains conjuring images, and along with the images – new meanings. Paul Ricoeur positioned imagination as linguistic at its roots, where language comes before the image and is necessary for any speculation and emergence of new meanings.[1] From this perspective, language is a catalyst for the emergence of images and consequently, meanings, and as such, it has the power to become a catalyst for design. Ricoeur made an urgent case for fiction being capable of changing reality, "(…) in the sense that it both 'invents' and 'discovers' it."[2]

This close, and to some extent mysterious relationship, between image and language (fiction, narrative), is at the core of imagination, the driving force of the design process.

"Imagination at work – in a work – produces itself as a world."[3] – writes Ricoeur, his words echoed by Hélène Frichot and Naomi Stead:

> Architects and fiction writers share much the same ambition: to imagine new worlds into being. Whether situated in the past, present or future, or layered as complex spatio-temporal strata,

DOI: 10.4324/9781003258933-1

architects and writers of fiction describe and document these
worlds, subsequently inviting others to occupy them.[4]

This affinity between writers and architects as world-builders widely
reverberates in the literature discussing the relationship between language (fiction) and architecture. Klaske Havik and Angeliki Sioli,
one of the authors in this volume, argue for the importance of literary
imagination in architectural education in these words:

> Through such literary devices as metaphor, imagination is
> seen as an agent in the creation of meaning in and through lan-
> guage, which Ricoeur calls "semantic innovation."[5] Following
> Ricoeur, we argue that imagination is more than the mere pro-
> duction of images, but rather the capacity to invent and see new
> worlds—and this is done first and foremost through language
> and narration.[6]

As world builders, writers, and architects engage with the world and
imagine it anew, therefore, the use of literary methods in design process and as research tools in architectural and urban explorations
should not be surprising, and indeed, it is an already established
and wide-ranging discussion. The realm of language, however, is not
considered a natural habitat of architects who traditionally prefer
visual forms of communication. For architects, there is a reluctance
to cross the divide between writing and drawing, a turn to writing
is often perceived as a betrayal of what is truly important in architectural practice: drawing, and eventually, building. You can hear
this attitude in Alvar Aalto's famous, not entirely serious statement,
almost teasing all "writing" architects:

> The Creator created paper for drawing architecture on. Everything
> else is, at least for my part, to misuse paper.[7]

In the same text, Aalto also reflected on his pedagogical struggles
caused by his reluctance to explain how to create good art. Hiding
behind the somewhat defensive, or simply honest, "I don't know,"
Aalto is half-joking in his answer, conceding that it is a serious matter to not know. By not answering, Aalto was standing his ground
in defence of his intuitive approach to architecture that in his view,
didn't need theorisation, nor justification.[8] His not entirely serious
answer reveals a common attitude in the profession valuing images
over words, and ultimately, buildings, over images.

And yet, architecture habitually forays into other disciplinary territories, always on the lookout for new ways of expression and understanding of the world. It is almost an established tradition in architecture to explore beyond its disciplinary boundaries, and constantly probe and redefine its field of exploration in search for inspiration and better understanding of its own practices and tools. Design studios in architecture schools are particularly important spaces of experimentation, where new ideas are tested with students who encounter them for the first time, allowing for the discussion to develop without sliding into established trajectories. The experimental nature of the design studio and the risk associated with all creative projects puts the architectural pedagogy at the forefront of experimentation in architecture, opening new avenues for research and practice. In the pedagogical context, the exploration of the relationship between space and language opens new directions in the discussion on a wide range of issues, including the organisation of the design studio, creative learning process, and value of interdisciplinary explorations.

The exploration of the relationship between architecture (space) and language (narrative, literary methods) is a well-established discussion, offering a firm theoretical foundation for in-studio experiments. Rooted in the Lefebvrian tradition of understanding space as a social construct,[9] and following Doreen Massey's characterisation of space as: "(...) open, multiple and relational, unfinished and always becoming (...),"[10] this discussion examines space using a matrix of literary methods and linguistic experiments, exploring relationships of space, time, meaning, perception, cognition, and imagination.

The role of narrative and its relationship with space and meaning[11] as discussed by Sophia Psarra; Klaske Havik's[12] explorations of the role of literature as a tool in understanding and creating of space, and finally, the ficto-critical writing taking an increasingly prominent role in architectural research as used by Jane Rendell,[13] Hélène Frichot[14] or Katja Grillner[15] among many others demonstrate the breadth of this discussion.

A recent book edited by Angeliki Sioli and Yoonchun Jung[16] brings together authors exploring the role of literature in architecture, academic research, architectural pedagogy centring the lived experience of place and championing the literary imagination in search for an alternative, ethically concerned architectural practice rooted in deep understanding of place and lived experience. Another line of inquiry, far beyond the scope of this book, is the discussion on the relationship between the city and literature, just to mention recent publications such as "Cities and literature"[17] by Malcom Miles, and two anthologies: "Research Companion to Architecture, Literature and the City" edited by Jonathan Charley,[18] and "Exploring the Spatiality of the City Across Cultural Texts. Narrating Spaces, Reading Urbanity" by Martin Kindermann and Rebekka Rohleder.[19] It is also important to note "writing" architects, those undeterred by Alvar Aalto's seemingly dismissive attitude towards writing: John Hejduk, Bernard Tschumi, Rem Koolhaas, Nigel Coates or Peter Zumthor,[20] and more recently Dorte Mandrup,[21] again one of many others.

Each chapter in this book situates its explorations within a wider discussion, carefully choosing its footing and offering a range of applied methods based on the ideas exploring the relationship between language and space. The chapters started as conference presentations during the Teaching – Learning – Research Design and Environments AMPS (Architecture, Media, Politics, Society) virtual conference in December 2020, hosted by Manchester School of Architecture. The pedagogical perspectives presented in the book offer a glimpse into the performance of those ideas when tested in a live and, to some extent, unpredictable, setting of the architecture school.

The two main themes of this book reflected in its title, catalysts and tensions, define how the literary methods are used in the pedagogies described by the authors. *Catalysts* refers to the use of the literary imagination as a catalyst for design projects and processes. This theme is the most evident in the first three chapters of the book in which the authors describe projects using literature and narrative as design tools that shape assignments and studio structures. This theme focusses on the role of narrative as a tool in design process and raises questions of the sources of imagination and the methods of stimulating it through literary methods.

The second theme, *Tensions,* identifies how spatial design pedagogy using narrative creatively exploits the gap between the world, as built and experienced, and its description through the written word. The act of translation is a key notion for this theme. As space is "translated" into images, images are then described with words, which in turn prompt new images and meanings to emerge, then again, closing the circle, may be transformed into space. From this perspective, the design process is a chain of acts of translation, each change from language to image full of potential to produce new meanings. In this process, which is mostly unconscious and subliminal, the unspoken and the barely acknowledged come to the surface in force, directing the design decisions, but revealing themselves only through a rigorous and in-depth investigation.

The result is a volume discussing a wide range of approaches to interdisciplinary design education exploring the opportunities and challenges of using narrative, literary imagination, and linguistic experimentation in architectural education. Through examples of student projects, this book examines boundaries of architectural education using linguistic and literary methods to support, reshape, and deconstruct the creative process. In the course of this book, we visit two architecture schools in North America, two in Europe, and one in India, demonstrating the wide reach and diversity of literary methods in architectural education.

Anuradha Chatterjee (Manipal University Jaipur, India) opens the book with a deep dive into the design studio with a non-linear structure, where a literary text was used to explore rhizomatic, non-hierarchical, and non-linear design thinking. Written from a feminist standpoint, this chapter describes an ambitious and challenging design studio setting, where hierarchies were dismantled and power was distributed between all participants to create a truly feminist learning environment. A traditional linear and tightly controlled design process was replaced with a rhizomatic and exploratory model, where letting go of control, embracing uncertainty, and risk were defining conditions of the process.

Students in Chatterjee's studio collaboratively read and then retold to each other "On the Banks of the Mayyazhi," a novel by M. Mukundan. In this co-reading and retelling process, students constructed a shared narrative of the site through the text, and then captured it through spatial experiments. The experimental and probing nature of this studio carefully engaged with the complex history of Mahé, a small town on the Malabar coast of India and an ex-French colony, allowing for a deep understanding of historical and cultural factors shaping the project site.

The studio's ambition was to educate a new type of a creative practitioner, one thriving in collaboration, capable of embracing the unknowable, always learning and never satisfied with just one point of view. The feminist perspective shapes Chatterjee's pedagogy and when applied in design studio pedagogy, it has the potential to disrupt patriarchal and hierarchical structures embedded in architectural education, and in result, empower students to find their own voice and expression beyond those structures.

In Chapter 2, Anca Matyiku (University of Cincinnati, US) explores how engagement with literature can propel the imagination in the process of design while also placing it in the contextual matrix of politics, environment, and social bonds underpinning all design decisions. Through the story of Billy the Kid, the infamous cattle robber, students revisited the local history and the myth-making of the American West. The project, although rooted in history, actively engaged with contemporary issues of homelessness, the concept of illegality of people and marginalisation.

Matyiku positions her pedagogical experiments in the context of Hans-Georg Gadamer's philosophical hermeneutics and frames design process as a dialogic experimentation, constantly engaging with the implicit and elusive aspects of design, allowing them to come to the fore and inform design decisions. They include not only designer's own biases and tacit forms of knowledge, but also undefined and somewhat mysterious "hunches and intuitions." An insightful design process uncovers those hidden powers and opens access to those important, but difficult to capture forms of knowledge, adding depth and self-reflection to design explorations.

For Matyiku, the use of literary imagination in architectural education has an ethical dimension, as she argues for "culturally conscientious architecture," positioning architecture in a wider cultural context, linking the broadening of horizons and cultural contextualisation with architecture sensitive to its position within wider cultural and social networks. She understands culturally conscientious design as an act capable of capturing elusive and implicit aspects of design, simultaneously revealing and incorporating them into the contextual understanding of architecture.

In Chapter 3, Angeliki Sioli (Delft University of Technology, the Netherlands) and Kristen Kelsch (Louisiana State University, US) focus on one of the most fundamental parts of architectural design process: the act of drawing. The authors explore how the cultivation of students' literary imagination has the potential to shape their perception of space, and subsequently its representation in their drawings. Following literary philosopher Elaine Scarry,[22] Sioli and Kelsch use the distinction between active and passive engagement with representations of spatial conditions.

The active engagement occurs in the act of reading, which engages imagination through the activation of the complex network of linguistic associations. In this perspective, the engagement with language is an active and creative process, contrasted to the passive consumption of images. This passivity is perceived by Sioli and Kelsch as an obstacle in the architecture education, particularly at the early stages of the design project, as the passive consumption of images can be a hindering factor in a creative process limiting students' imagination and horizon of expression. To jumpstart the process, they used literary texts by authors from different cultural backgrounds and times. The texts ranged from Haruki Murakami's "The Windup Bird Chronicle" (1995), through Franz Kafka's short story "The Burrow" (1931), Edgar Allan Poe's short story "The Masque of the Red Death" from 1842, to the "I hold a wolf by the ears" (2020) collection of stories by Laura van den Berg, among others.

Students also experimented with the body of text itself and were encouraged to manipulate it through drawing, searching for new meanings emerging from the collision of language and drawing. The aim was to create an intimate, but visual connection with literature, and as the texts contained descriptions of spaces, the exercise focussed students' attention on observation, the crucial part of any design project. The act of reading was accompanied by quick sketches directly on the pages of the chosen texts, creating another layer of understanding and interpretation in the process of reading. Using the art work "A Humument: A Treated Victorian Novel," by Tom Phillips[23] students continued their contextual re-reading of the text, adding more visual layers to the text, deconstructing it, and creating new meanings. This activity allowed them to freely engage with the text, breaking the boundary between the body of text and drawing, releasing creative potential when exploring the written word as a visual entity that can be manipulated and its meaning reinterpreted and expanded in the process.

The theme of *Tensions* defines the last two chapters of the book in which the authors focus on pedagogical approaches exploring the gaps between the tangible spatial realities of the world and the limitations of language attempting to capture it in its full complexity and richness.

Chapter 4 (Kasia Nawratek, Manchester School of Architecture, UK) discusses an interdisciplinary and collaborative project exploring the intersection of mapping, poetry, and film making. Using Mikhail Bakhtin's idea of polyphony,[24] the project explored the relationship between space and language, harnessing the creative potential of the gap between the world and its description.

The spatial focus of the project was on spaces eluding a precise definition and known as drosscape,[25] the Third Landscape[26] and Edgelands as introduced by Marion Shoard[27] and explored by poets Michael Symmons Roberts and Paul Farley.[28] They are the urban wastelands, undefined city edges, unattended and forgotten liminal spaces, existing on the edge of the consciousness of the city dwellers.

Their elusiveness and the uncanny ability to hide in plain sight, allowed for linguistic explorations, where the impossibility of one, definite description led to the multiplicity of subjective approaches revealing the subversive potential of language.

The polyphonic method allowed for alternative narratives to emerge, undermining and eroding the boundaries of the monologic capitalist narrative of precisely calculated value, situating Edgelands as the last spatial defence against the all-encompassing capitalist narrative in the city. The act of translation, understood not only as a process of mediation between space and language, but also as a conversation between various modes of representation and communication, underpinned all explorations undertaken in this project bringing to the fore the linguistic diversity among students and thus situating the studio in a wider cultural context.

As Nawratek argues for multiplication of narratives in her work, Nicolai Bo Andersen and Victor Boye Julebæk (Royal Danish Academy, Denmark) skip the translation between image and language entirely in search for a direct connection between made and spoken matter. In Chapter 5, they discuss the tension between the (physical) experience of buildings and cities and the spoken (verbal) vocabulary used to describe it. Rooted in the so-called new phenomenology as developed by Hermann Schmitz, their focus is on the body as the basis of human experience.[29] They reflect on the disparity between materiality and the language that is used by professionals to describe it. Through the act of making, students explored the embodied, tacit knowledge gained through manual production of concrete samples, which was then captured through a set of standardised descriptions. This approach aims to capture a linguistic description of tangible and observable phenomena of materiality in order to enhance the understanding of materiality as a driving force in design process.

Andersen and Julebæk position materiality in architecture as a language itself, arguing for a more systematic approach to the relationship between materiality and experienced effects. Following Juhani Pallasmaa,[30] they argue for a connection among language, embodied knowledge, and architecture, in order to steer away from mere image making, and focus back on an embodied experience engaging all senses. The act of making performed by students in the studio becomes a shared experience, where tutors and students participate in an experiment that establishes communication based on the experienced material effects, creating a meaningful connection to the world, and positioning the learning and teaching process as a creative act.

As evidenced in this book, language can be used as a catalyst, a prompt, a way of jumpstarting design process, where the linguistic becomes visual, and the implied becomes specific. The act of translation between the linguistic and the visual can reveal the hidden powers forcing the designer's hand, uncovering not only biases and preconceptions, but through an introspection, opening the design process to include a critical evaluation of solutions and paths taken to reach them. When approached this way, design process has the potential to delve deeper, reject an easy route, and point to a more exploratory path. Inevitably, the pedagogies using this positioning gain a strong ethical perspective.

This is particularly evident in pedagogies discussed by Chatterjee, Matyiku, and Nawratek, where their design studio pedagogies are synergic with their ethical perspectives on design. They are important examples, as they highlight that any recalibration of the design process has a direct impact on the organisation of the design studio and the learning environment it creates. Their pedagogical practices demonstrate, how design process and pedagogy of the design studio are intricately linked, and should be understood not so much as reflections of each other, but more as one, synergic methodology manifesting itself through both the design process and the studio organisation. In other words, any desired values underpinning the design process need to be also reflected in the studio pedagogy and delivery, so that design proposals match the tools used to shape them.

This synergy is best demonstrated in the project led by Nawratek, where Bakhtin's polyphony is both used as the theoretical framework for the project and the basis for the pedagogical approach, where all voices are given space and recognition even in a literal sense, as the linguistic diversity of the student group is used as the creative resource and, at the same time, an empowering tool. This linguistic richness, including various languages and accents, represents the variety of voices that are often expected to conform to a narrow linguistic and cultural norm, reflecting the profession which at its highest levels of success and recognition, rarely deviates from a white, patriarchal template.

Nawratek also makes a case for architectural pedagogy as a creative practice, where design studio becomes a space for a community of practice, setting students and tutors on a shared creative journey. Their trajectories are different, but when positioned right, a sense of shared exploration can be equally valuable to all involved in the process. This can only be achieved in a learning environment with flattened hierarchies following the polyphonic and dialogic approach rooted in Bakhtin's philosophy. From this perspective, the role of the tutor is to share their tools and help students to sharpen and build theirs, but the challenge lays far beyond the expected set of skills that students are expected to gain at the end of the project. This also implies the learning process shouldn't be perceived as a completed chapter confined to one project, but a journey stretching far into the future. This long-term positioning of goals can significantly diminish the fear of failure, and in turn open students to the idea of growth and creative journey which does not conform to predetermined trajectories of steady and predictable growth.

The positioning of architectural pedagogy as a creative act is, to some extent, echoed by Andersen and Julebæk, who see their pedagogical practice as a dialogic process between tutors and students, where a direct engagement with experienced material effects has the ability to transform and affect both students and tutors.

For Matyiku and Chatterjee, the contextually sensitive approach defines their pedagogy methods. Through rooting the design process in the complex web of contextual interdependencies and developing immersive methods of site analysis, building on deep connections with the place, the literary methods used in these studios aim to create a personal connection with the site, playing on the emotional investment made in the process of creative engagement with a place and characters inhabiting it.

The emotional aspect of design work is often obscured by the academic language used to describe it.[31] And yet, it is impossible not to detect it under seemingly detached descriptions of student work. The outright feminist positioning of the design studio led by Chatterjee allows for this emotional dimension to be captured by its retelling, giving space to this often-overlooked component of the design process.

As there is no creative endeavour without risk and fear of failure, the learning environment of the design studio is charged with strong emotions. The feminist perspective makes space for the acknowledgment of the emotional labour associated with assisting with this process, giving a deeper, and more accurate insight into the pedagogical processes taking place in the design studio. Matyiku's deep reach into the forces lurking just underneath the surface of the conscious reveals not only tacit knowledge and harness the creative potential of intuitions and hunches but also uncovers hidden biases and preconceptions, disturbing an established order and students' understanding of the world. This cannot be a painless and emotionless process. Chatterjee's and Matyiku's design studios are challenging learning environments, supportive but at the same time confronting students with their own preconceptions and biases. To effectively, and sensitively manage the tension created in such charged learning environment, steering the projects into successful completion is the true skill of design studio educators. It is a line of inquiry that does not fit within the remit of this book, but I would like to acknowledge it, as even if not specifically expressed, it can be detected in the background, waiting to be expanded and explored further in the future.

What emerges as a side effect of engaged pedagogies, is the potential to disrupt embedded structures of dominance in the architectural pedagogy and change the way young architects understand their position in the design process, and as a consequence, the role of the profession in the society. This positions design studios in architecture schools as very influential, having a direct impact on the profession and beyond. With the climate crisis threatening, the very existence of humanity and triggering a domino effect of social and economic upheaval, the pedagogies of inclusivity, curiosity, contextual sensitivity, and self-reflection provide a much-needed rethink of the design studio organisation and structure.

The methods discussed in this book are practical and applied, demonstrating the usefulness of literary and linguistic approaches in architectural education. It is, however, important to note that they can be challenging for educators, as they require a firm grasp of the theoretical context and a clear sense of purpose that they are meant to serve. The examples in the book not only demonstrate the careful positioning of the presented methods but also reflect on the unpredictable nature of pedagogy in creative subjects, highlighting the experimental nature of design studio and the challenges that come with it.

Although international in scope, the projects discussed in this book share the ambition of keeping the discussion about the disciplinary boundaries of architecture alive and prove the important role of architecture schools as laboratories and testing grounds for ideas. This book offers a glimpse into the lively and experimental world of architectural education, and even with just five chapters, the breadth of explorations is far-reaching and exploratory, which only raises the question, what else might be happening in the field. Therefore, I believe this book will be useful for innovators in architectural education, not only those who will see connections between their pedagogy practices and the methods discussed in the book, but also those who may seek to expand and refresh their teaching practice to incorporate literary methods. I would consider this a success, if this book inspired a creative practitioner, an architect, designer, artist, or a writer, to make teaching a part of their creative journey.

The collaborative nature of design studio in architecture schools offers a unique opportunity for interdisciplinary cross-pollination and can be equally nourishing for all involved. When entering the studio, a collaborator from another discipline takes on a double role – of someone sharing a different point of view and toolkit used in the craftsmanship of their discipline, and of someone who needs to learn with the students, exposed to the unfamiliar disciplinary environment. A mere presence of a practitioner from another discipline disturbs the embedded hierarchies of the design studio, raising the question of who learns from whom, and opening the new trajectories of exploration, not only allowing new questions to be asked, but also questioning established ways of thinking and doing. Perhaps this book will inspire educators in architecture to seek those interdisciplinary connections more actively and open their design studios to outsiders bringing new ideas, tools, and perspectives.

Another group, that this book hopes to resonate with, are students. Mainly architecture students, but other design-based disciplines with an established design studio culture, may find it interesting too. Some insight into the mysterious creative process might be particularly useful, validating students' own struggles with creativity. The fear of blank page is a recognised phenomenon, as Angeliki Sioli and Kristen Kelsch demonstrate in their chapter. They also address the oversaturation with images experienced in our visually oriented culture and recognise that it can be detrimental for students at the start of their creative journeys still formulating their individual visual languages and modes of expression. In this book, you can find examples of how to use the written word, narrative, poetry, and literature to feed your imagination.

Architectural education is constantly striving to remain relevant and respond to contemporary challenges. It also strives to keep up with the profession and prepare students for its challenges. These, however ambitious goals, are not its only focus, because as evidenced in this book, architectural educators care deeply about students' development as creative individuals. The learning environment they create is not meant to bring short-term gains but builds a strong foundation for a life-long creative practice. It also demonstrates how architectural education recognises its role in shaping informed and sensitive citizens, actively responding to the challenges of the so called "real world." But perhaps, this is a false dichotomy and academia *is* a part of the world, actively co-creating it and engaging with its ever-changing complexities. Perhaps there is no such a thing as the ivory tower of academy, looking over the busy landscape of the so-called real world, with academics solemnly instructing reluctant students on the ways of the world below.

To close this introduction, I leave you with an image of a tower, that is not there.

Notes

1 Richard Kearney, "Paul Ricoeur and the hermeneutic imagination." *Philosophy & Social Criticism* 14, no. 2 (1988): 115–145.
2 Paul Ricoeur, "The Function of Fiction in Shaping Reality," in *A Ricoeur Reader* (University of Toronto Press, 2016), 117–136.
3 Ricoeur, *A Ricoeur Reader,* 123.
4 Hélène Frichot and Naomi Stead, "Waking Ideas from Their Sleep: An Introduction to Ficto-Critical Writing in and of Architecture," in *Writing Architectures: Ficto-Critical Approaches,* eds. Hélène Frichot and Naomi Stead (London: Bloomsbury Publishing, 2020), 11.
5 Paul Ricoeur, *Hermeneutics and the Human Sciences* (Cambridge: Cambridge University Press, 1981).
6 Klaske Havik and Angeliki Sioli, "Stories for architectural imagination." *Journal of Architectural Education* 75, no. 2 (2021), accessed January 15, 2022, doi: 10.1080/10464883.2021.1947670.
7 Alvar Aalto, "Instead of an article." *Drawing Matter*, June 3, 2020, accessed January 15, 2022, https://drawingmatter.org/aalto-instead-of-an-article/.
8 Rika Devos, Mil De Kooning, Scott Poole, and Pia Sarpaneva, "The Merging of Proportion Theory, Morphology and 'National' Imagery in Fifties Modern Architecture: The Pietilä Pavilion at Expo 58," *Contribution or Confusion: Architecture and the Influence of other Fields of Inquiry. Proceedings of the 2003 ACSA International Conference*, pp. 15–22. ACSA Press, 2004, 16.
9 Henri Lefebvre, *The Production of Space,* trans. Donald Nicholson-Smith (Oxford: Blackwell, 1991).
10 Doreen Massey and Doreen B. Massey, *For Space* (London: Sage, 2005), 59.
11 Sophia Psarra, *Architecture and Narrative: The Formation of Space and Cultural Meaning* (London: Routledge, 2009).
12 Klaske Maria Havik, *Urban Literacy: Reading and Writing Architecture* (Rotterdam: NAi Publishers, 2014). Klaske Havik, Susana Oliveira, Jorge Mejia Hernandez, Mike Schafer, and Mark Proosten. *Writingplace: Investigations in Architecture and Literature* (Rotterdam: nai010 uitgevers, 2016).
13 Jane Rendell, *Art and Architecture: A Place Between* (London: IB Tauris, 2006).
14 Hélène Frichot, "Stealing into Deleuze's Baroque House," in *Deleuze and Space,* eds. Ian Buchanan and Gregg Lambert (Edinburgh: University of Edinburgh Press, 2005), 61–79.

15 Katja Grillner, "Ramble, linger and gaze," PhD dissertation (Stockholm: KTH, 2000).
16 Angeliki Sioli and Yoonchun Jung, eds., *Reading Architecture: Literary Imagination and Architectural Experience* (New York: Routledge, 2018).
17 Malcolm Miles, *Cities and Literature* (London: Routledge, 2018).
18 Jonathan Charley, ed., *Research Companion to Architecture, Literature and the City* (London: Routledge, 2018).
19 Martin Kindermann and Rebekka Rohleder, eds., *Exploring the Spatiality of the City Across Cultural Texts. Narrating Spaces, Reading Urbanity* (Cham: Palgrave Macmillan, 2020).
20 Some notable publications by 'writing' architects:
    Nigel Coates, *Narrative Architecture* (Chichester: John Wiley & Sons, 2012).
    Peter Zumthor, *Thinking Architecture* (Basel: Birkhäuser, 2010).
    Rem Koolhaas, *Delirious New York: A Retroactive Manifesto for Manhattan* (Rotterdam: 010 Publishers, 1994).
    Bernard Tschumi, *Event-Cities: Praxis* (Cambridge, MA: MIT press, 1994).
21 Dorte Mandrup, "Creating Change with Impact: An Architect's Manifesto," in *Everything Needs to Change. Architecture and the Climate Emergency*, eds. Sofie Pelsmakers and Nick Newman (London: RIBA Publishing, 2021), 1.
22 Elaine Scarry, *Dreaming by the Book* (Princeton: Princeton University Press, 2001), 76.
23 Tom Phillips, *A Humument: A Treated Victorian Novel* (New York: Thames and Hudson, 1997).
24 Andrew Robinson, "In Theory Bakhtin: Dialogism, Polyphony and Heteroglossia," *Ceasefire,* July 29, 2011, accessed January 14, 2022, https://ceasefiremagazine.co.uk/in-theory-bakhtin-1/.
25 Alan Berger, *Drosscape. Wasting Land in Urban America* (New York: Princeton Architectural Press, 2006).
26 Gilles Clément, "The Third Landscape," accessed January 15, 2021, http://www.gillesclement.com/art-454-tit-The-Third-Landscape.
27 Marion Shoard, "Edgelands," *The Land Magazine,* accessed January 15, 2022, https://www.thelandmagazine.org.uk/articles/Edgelands.
28 Paul Farley and Michel Symmons Roberts, *Edgelands* (London: Vintage Books, 2012).
29 Hermann Schmitz, *New Phenomenology* (Milan: Mimesis International, 2019).
30 Juhani Pallasmaa, *The Eyes of the Skin* (Chichester: John Wiley & Sons, 2005), 31.
31 The academic language proves to be challenging for the author, as evidenced by the switch from the first-person narrative at the beginning of this text to the third person she uses to write about her own work. It seems that the academic convention requiring a neutral position, despite normalising writing in the first person by feminist human geographer Doreen Massey (again, among others), is still too much of a barrier for the author to overcome in this text. The switch from the first person to third is awkward but highlights something important. Together with the acknowledgment of emotion as an integral part of any creative activity, such as writing, be it academic or creative, but also of

pedagogy when understood as a creative practice, it highlights the need for deeper examination of voices in the academic setting, and what they may tell us. In simple terms, the "how" proves to be as important as "what" is being said.

Bibliography

Aalto, Alvar. "Instead of an article." *Drawing Matter*, June 3, 2020. Accessed January 15, 2022, https://drawingmatter.org/aalto-instead-of-an-article/.

Berger, Alan. Drosscape. *Wasting Land in Urban America*. New York, NY: Princeton Architectural Press, 2006.

Charley, Jonathan, ed. *Research Companion to Architecture, Literature and the City*. London: Routledge, 2018.

Clément, Gilles. "The Third Landscape" Accessed January 15, 2021, http://www.gillesclement.com/art-454-tit-The-Third-Landscape.

Coates, Nigel. *Narrative Architecture*. Chichester: John Wiley & Sons, 2012.

Devos, Rika, Mil De Kooning, Scott Poole, and Pia Sarpaneva. "The Merging of Proportion Theory, Morphology and 'National' Imagery in Fifties Modern Architecture: The Pietilä Pavilion at Expo 58." In *Contribution or Confusion: Architecture and the Influence of other Fields of Inquiry. Proceedings of the 2003 ACSA International Conference*, pp. 15–22. Helsinki: ACSA Press, 2004.

Farley, Paul and Michael Symmons Roberts. *Edgelands*. London: Vintage Books, 2012.

Frichot, Hélène. "Stealing into Deleuze's Baroque House." In *Deleuze and Space*, edited by Ian Buchanan and Gregg Lambert, 61–79. Edinburgh: University of Edinburgh Press, 2005.

Frichot, Hélène and Naomi Stead, eds. *Writing Architectures: Ficto-Critical Approaches*. London: Bloomsbury Publishing, 2020.

Grillner, Katja. *Ramble, Linger and Gaze*. Stockholm: KTH, 2000.

Havik, Klaske. *Urban Literacy: Reading and Writing Architecture*. Rotterdam: nai010, 2014.

Havik, Klaske and Angeliki Sioli. "Stories for Architectural Imagination." *Journal of Architectural Education* 75, no. 2 (2021), accessed January 15, 2022, doi: 10.1080/10464883.2021.1947670.Havik, Klaske, Susana Oliveira, Jorge Mejia Hernandez, Mike Schafer, and Mark Proosten. *Writingplace: Investigations in Architecture and Literature*. Rotterdam: nai010, 2016.

Kearney, Richard. "Paul Ricoeur and the hermeneutic imagination." *Philosophy & Social Criticism* 14, no. 2 (1988): 115–145.

Kindermann, Martin and Rebekka Rohleder, eds. *Exploring the Spatiality of the City Across Cultural Texts: Narrating Spaces, Reading Urbanity*. Cham: Palgrave Macmillan, 2020.

Koolhaas, Rem. *Delirious New York: A Retroactive Manifesto for Manhattan*. Rotterdam: 010 Publishers, 1994.

Lefebvre, H. and Donald Nicholson-Smith. *The Production of Space*, Vol. 142. Blackwell: Oxford, 1991.

Lefebvre, Henri. *The Production of Space*. Translated by Donald Nicholson-Smith. Oxford: Blackwell, 1991.

Malcolm Miles. *Cities and Literature*. London: Routledge, 2018.

Mandrup, Dorte. "Creating Change with Impact: An Architect's Manifesto." In *Everything Needs to Change: Architecture and the Climate Emergency*, edited by Sofie Pelsmakers and Nick Newman, 1–11. London: RIBA Publishing, 2021.

Massey, Doreen and Doreen B. Massey. *For Space*. London: Sage, 2005.

Pallasmaa, Juhani. *The Eyes of the Skin*. Chichester: John Wiley & Sons, 2005.

Phillips, Tom. *A Humument: A Treated Victorian Novel*. New York, NY: Thames and Hudson, 1997.

Psarra, Sophia. *Architecture and Narrative: The Formation of Space and Cultural Meaning*. London: Routledge, 2009.

Rendell, Jane. *Art and Architecture: A Place Between*. London: IB Tauris, 2006.

Ricoeur, Paul. "The Function of Fiction in Shaping Reality." In *A Ricoeur Reader*, 117–136. Toronto: University of Toronto Press, 2016.

Scarry, Elaine. *Dreaming by the Book*. Princeton, NJ: Princeton University Press, 2001.

Schmitz, Hermann. *New Phenomenology*. Milan: Mimesis International, 2019.

Shoard, Marion. "Edgelands." *The Land Magazine*. Accessed January 15, 2022, https://www.thelandmagazine.org.uk/articles/edgelands.

Sioli, Angeliki and Yoonchun Jung, eds. *Reading Architecture: Literary Imagination and Architectural Experience*. New York, NY: Routledge, 2018.

Tschumi, Bernard. *Event-Cities: Praxis*. Cambridge, MA: MIT press, 1994.

Zumthor, Peter. *Thinking Architecture*. Basel: Birkhäuser, 2010.

1 In between fiction and space

Feminist studio pedagogy (of letting go)

Anuradha Chatterjee

Critical intersections: Feminist pedagogies and studio methodologies

This chapter brings into conversation my trajectory as a feminist academic practitioner through the lens of a studio project. Feminist pedagogy is defined by Carolyn M. Shrewsbury as learning and teaching processes that aim to create a "liberatory environment," where some power is shared, and which eventually aim to undertake a "transformation of the academy."[1] Feminist pedagogies initiate the dismantling of practices of power and domination, and create "empowering classrooms," where students can find their voice.[2] In essence, argue Robbin D. Crabtree, David Alan Sapp, and Adela C. Licona, it is a "movement against hegemonic educational practices that tacitly accept or more forcefully reproduce an oppressively gendered, classed, racialized, and androcentric social order."[3] It is, argues Julie Brown, also interested in challenging the authoritative, patriarchal structures in education. This involves not only transforming pedagogical practices but also patriarchal knowledge systems and canons embedded in the curriculum and course content.[4] The urgent need for this in architecture is presented by Torsten Lange and Emily Eliza Scott, as they make a timely case for enacting substantive change in the discipline of architecture, and a careful reconsideration of the ways "'architectural' knowledge is produced and reproduced."[5] Very incisively, they note that architecture is a "notoriously conservative discipline with roots in the long nineteenth century, all too often clings to traditional notions of individual mastery, genius, and autonomy, while also maintaining deeply hierarchical and patriarchal structures."[6] They mount a timely call to "meaningful 'troublemaking' in the architectural discipline" through "alternatives to normative forms of knowledge production," which is the space within which I work.[7]

DOI: 10.4324/9781003258933-2

As a feminist academic practitioner, who has refused to stay "in her place," in architectural history and theory, and who has "dared" to work across, through to architectural design studios, as an outsider, a dilettante, "practicing" architecture in the academy, not industry, I have come to realise that there is something quite worrying about the designerly (and patriarchal) proclivity towards control. One of the key narratives that permeated a lot of the studios was how design was to know exactly what is happening and where, in a proposed space, building, precinct, and to be able to transform intent into articulation. The idea of chance, accident, not fully knowing or being in complete control of every corner of designed space was often dismissed, trivialised, and I suspect, feared. Not only is this indicative of a commercial imperative (as every square meter of built space is viewed essentially as a commodity constructed and purchased at a price) but it is also an undeclared position that views the unmapped or the unmappable with suspicion, as something that cannot be governed. Another aspect of studio pedagogies that I found problematic was the water-tight, process-orientated pedagogy and its "forward march," which did not seem liberating, forgiving, or feminist. Therefore, in my critique of power and control in and of architectural knowledges, and in considering feminist ways of knowing, I delve into "policed spaces" in architecture and consider other ways of proceeding, in studio.

At Avani Institute of Design, we explored the feminist pedagogy of "letting go," through studio project titled "Narrative, Sense and Space: Cultural Interpretation Centre, Mahé."[8] In collaboration with the studio team (Meenakshi Dubey, Vinod CP, and Shyam Gandhi) and a group of 36 students, we proposed a small-scale institutional building, which needed to engage the local and regional visitors in a shared, meaningful, and pluralistic cultural history, articulated through its functional (uses, inhabitations), interpretative (stories, histories, and narratives), and architectonic (material, spatial, experiential, both fleeting and enduring) programme. The feminist pedagogy of the studio was structured as differential intensities and speeds of navigating culture, context, site, architectonics, and affect. Intuitively, it was informed by the intersection of four complementary critiques in/of design: (1) design research, and its associated paradigms of inquiry, rigour, experimentation, and uncertainty; (2) critique of control in total design; (3) generative fragments as processes that help "activate conceptualisation processes"; and (4) rhizomatic, non-hierarchical, non-dualistic non-linear design thinking.

David Salomon's historical and theoretical survey of the rise of the research studio (and the end of design studio) explains that one of the key reason educators are moving away from design thesis to research studio is that students and staff are now seen as engaged in moving "away from independent explorations and toward the collective production of disciplinary knowledge."[9] Design as scholarship is really clarified by considering the distinction between research and science. Salomon explains this through the writings of Bruno Latour, as he notes the "affinity between research and design as similarly experimental, subjective, and political processes."[10] Through Latour's writings, Salomon argues for design (as research) as "uncertainty"; "warm, involving, and risky"; capable of provoking "controversies"; and engaging with "ideology, passions, and emotions."[11] Students are expected to engage in inquiries that negotiate project particulars with quest for knowledge; professional competence with speculation and invention, and "all the while advancing disciplinary knowledge." This is further elucidated by Helene Furjan who argues that design research should test the boundaries of the discipline, and subject pedagogical approaches to "new analyses, new techniques, and new theories."[12] Research within the context of design should be speculative and open to new opportunities, and a "generator of speculation and a reservoir for potentialities to be tapped," for "inclinations and hunches."[13] In the context of a studio with a common brief, the contribution to disciplinary knowledge is a collective set of insights that transcend the personal, to prompt theoretical reflections and ontological questions, concerning design and the act of designing.

The elements of risk and uncertainty in design research find resonance in the critique of control in design. This is relevant especially in the design of an interpretation centre, where a strong narrative and experiential programme could do disservice to the design of a democratic public space by undermining the agency of the visitor. To this end, it became important to reorient our studio towards the history and critique of total design, as presented by Mark Wigley in his 1998 essay "Whatever Happened to Total Design?"[14] While Wigley examined the history of total design (from Gropius to Venturi), which was "a fantasy about control, about architecture as control," he also argued that there is also "no such thing as non-totalizing design. All design is total design." However, he also argued that this "totalizing dream is always frustrated," and the "more one studies the totalizing images and narratives, the more one discovers parts of the architecture, the publication, or the history that have escaped or slipped the grip of those who so resolutely frame and present them." It is also relevant to this debate, and the studio, that the paradigm of total design is enhanced by architectural representations that are associated with a kind of gaze that are "neither neutral nor disinterested, and always invested in a certain politics of looking."[15] Damjan Jovanovic talks about an "orthographic gaze as well as a perspectival gaze," and especially the orthographic gaze, which enacts "total control" of the model space due its emphasis on the top and side view.[16] With that critique in mind, the studio considered fragments as a way to proceed.

We wanted to see whether and to what extent the design process could be a negotiation of designerly control, as well as the lack of it. We therefore borrowed from Karl Wallick's work with generative fragments. Wallick argues correctly: "We remember instances, elements, details. Rarely are the images and sensations in architectural experience comprehensive. The context of what we do as architects is always fragmentary even as it seeks to be resolved comprehensively."[17] He takes this further to formulate an approach to design which was based on developing sectional fragment models and joining them to compose the "whole." The entire objective was to discourage students from "pre-conceptualizing a holistic building form or designing the entire building as a schematic," and to not be in a position to conceptualise the entire building until the "eighth and final sectional model is constructed."[18] For Wallick, this is not a formalist premise, as he draws upon Ignasi de Sola-Morales's reflections on the condition of human existence as one of "estrangement," which structures our "erratic, nomadic perception of reality," such that reality is always "unfinished, the partial, and the cumulative," which also informs architecture.[19] For us, an additional reason for engaging with the idea of assemblage was to do with confounding the knowing eye in orthographic methods used to control gridded space.

And finally, to embrace the promise of design research whilst forfeiting designerly control and an architecture of wholeness, the studio was committed to a methodology, which was not designed as non-linear as such, but one that could absorb transgressive movements and shocks across its terrain. Randall Teal is right when he notes how the richness of design "gets diluted when design is imagined to be merely a series of iterations along a linear path."[20] This is exacerbated by the chronological weekly structure of the studio marked by sequential tasks and developmental stages, such that the conceptualisation invariably moves from two to three dimensional; not knowing to knowing; and virtual to real. This is what Teal would characterise as the "treelike view of design [which] is limited because, similar to a tree, it is slow moving, centred, hierarchical and grows from one monolithic 'trunk.'"[21] Instead, he offers Deleuze and Guttari's rhizome as a "more complete visualisation of the design process." The rhizome can be described as a network of things such that "any point of a rhizome can be connected to anything other and must be. This is very different from the tree or root, which plots a point, fixes an order."[22] However, as Teal explains, using rhizomatic thinking does not mean the "overturning of systems, but rather a recalibrating of practices," which "promotes complex visualisations while still incorporating the intelligibility of order and linearity."[23] The Cultural Interpretation Centre studio interwove these four strands into productive complexities, starting with the selection of the context and site.

City, history, fiction

We decided to position our inquiry and the studio project within Mahé (also known as Mayyazhi) for the contextual complexities and contradictions (some of them perhaps even irresolvable) it appeared to embody. Mahé is a small town, an ex-French colony on the Malabar Coast of India, adjacent to Kerala and within the Union Territory of Puducherry (see Figure 1.1). Mahé was named after French commander Bertrand Francois Mahe de La Bourdonnais (1699–1753).[24] The Mayyazhi river was central to the geopolitics of Mahé, as it "has a total course of about thirty-four miles from its origin in the forests of the Wayanad ghats to its merger with the Arabian sea," which enabled the "French to obtain the major share of spices produced in the kingdom of Kadathanad," and provide "easier accessibility to the hinterland."[25] Mahé was set up as a trading post by the French East India company in 1721; captured by the British in the French English War in 1761 and returned to France in 1763 under the Treaty of Paris; recaptured by the British in 1779 and returned to France

Figure 1.1 View of murals in Tagore Park, Mahé; Mahé River; and Mahé Breakwater.

Source: Photos by Anuradha Chatterjee.

in 1814, after which it remained with the French despite the British dominance of India in the 1850s, till Mahé's liberation through local rebellion in 1954.[26] In 1962, the transfer of power occurred, which led to the formation of the Union Territory of Pondicherry (now known as Puducherry), comprising ex-French settlements of Pondicherry, Karaikal, Mahé, and Yanam.

Mahé has had a long and complex history. The residents speak Malayalam, but they are not "Malayalis," and many people identify with France much more than identify with Kerala, or India. This is because, explains Sreya Ann Oommen, Mahé's cultural identity has emerged historically through the encounter between the people known as the *mayyazhikkar* and the people of Indo-French descent.[27] In addition, explains Animesh Rai, after 1963, several people (known as optants) opted to take up French citizenship. Rai notes that there are "currently approximately 8000 Indians of French nationality in the Union Territory of Pondicherry," of which "approximately 2000 are actually French speaking or have links with France through pensions."[28] Mahé's postcolonial identity, explains Oommen, was also informed by French assimilative policies focused on producing "fragmented identities" and preventing "absolute identity formulation," to "aid the harmonious coexistence of Mahéans," which ironically left many feeling homeless and without a sense of belonging.[29] Mahé is now infamous as a place where people from the state of Kerala come to buy cheap alcohol. Making use of Mahé's location within the Thalassery heritage tourism circuit, a Cultural Interpretation Centre was imagined – as a project that could stimulate and assist the process of rediscovery and re-inscription of historical and contemporary culture.

While the most obvious thing to do in a design studio is to make a physical visit to the site for context study, we deliberately started with a collective reading of M. Mukundan's 1974 Malayalam novel *Mayyazhippuzhayude Theerangalil*, translated by Gita Krishnankutty into English in 1999 as *On the Banks of the Mayyazhi*.[30] In "Aesthetics of Place," Jayalekshmi J. summarises the novel:

> A wave of nationalism lashed on the banks of Mayyazhi, when a group of determined men decides to release Mayyazhi from the clutches of the French invasion. The hero is a young man called Dasan who was born in French Mahe and educated in Pondicherry. Despite the fact that he was extended to an employment opportunity in the French administration and assistance for higher education in Paris, he rather joins the freedom

movement led by Gandhian Kanaran and is fascinated by communist ideology. A girl called Chandrika falls in love with him, however he can't to promise her a married life because of his commitment to the revolution. A French court sentences Dasan to 12 years of imprisonment, but Dasan away from imprisonment by walking across to the Indian Union. Very soon he returns to Mahe leading a gathering of volunteers and liberates Mahé from foreign rule. The French national flag is taken out and the Indian national flag is hoisted on government buildings. In spite of being a local hero, he struggles for his livelihood as he refuses to accept regular employment and join the mainstream lifestyle. His girlfriend is constrained by her parents to marry another man, so she commits suicide. Dasan also follows her way to reach the abode of the soul on the Velliyamkallu island on the Mahe coast.[31]

The historical-political fiction by Mukundan is used as a point of entry into Mahé as a place. Instead of diving into the "real" and present Mahé, we wanted students to inhabit the fictive-material space of Mahé (as constructed in the novel) and understand that the characters of the novel may be as real as the people who lived/live in Mahé, and to understand town's cultural, political, and linguistic complexities. Swapna Gopinath argues:

> Mukundan's novels on Mayyazhi are perfect examples for this treatment of history in fiction. The novels are shaped with the history of Mahe as the backdrop and the changes that take place in the small principality become the canvas on which the characters are painted with a touch of humaneness and pathos. The colonial culture and its disintegration as well as the mind frame of the natives are all faithfully drawn in the saga of Mayyazhi.[32]

Gopinath also quotes K. Satchidanandan who claims:

> On the *Banks of the Mayyazhi* is a fictional record—often with a strong factual basis—of the struggles and travails of a people caught in the trauma of transition that catches them unawares, pleases, baffles and horrifies them at the same time .... Mukundan's narrative does not however stop with the political aspect of the anti-colonial struggle: he delves deep into the minds and lives of his characters and minutely records the impact of the struggle on individual destinies.[33]

It is also no coincidence then that the walkway through Mahé's Tagore Park, leading up to the riverside walkway, features a continuous wall adorned with mural made of relief bronze sculptures, of scenes from Mukundan's novel.

Fictive-material city/space in the novel

The studio methodology was not just experimental, it was also collaborative. Instead of reading the novel on their own and in its entirety, each student read one chapter and narrated it to their peers in class. Not only was the novel read, but it was also retold. The process of reading, remembering, telling, listening, and asking questions was used to create a shared memory of the novel, much like oral history, which Della Pollock describes as the "process of making history in dialogue," in that it is "performative," "cocreative, co-embodied, specially framed, contextually and intersubjectively contingent."[34] In some sense, this also reconstructs the story or the stories within the novel, creating a new original, a new novel. We recognised that the process of reading, remembering, and inhabiting the novel is an affective and a spatial act. The notion of fictional space is explored by Anette Arlander in her performance work, wherein she explains this as "textual space, the places of action, their transformations and meanings, and potential interpretations created onstage."[35] To this end, real space is where something is performed, and it "specifies and gives detail to fictional space and, on the other hand, it creates new fiction."[36] Therefore, the studio proposed that students select five to six significant episodes, moments from the chapters they read and transform them into a pictorial representation in the form of a graphic tile. Each tile is a spatial vignette with three attributes: (1) event, (2) spatial quality or setting, and (3) emotion or atmosphere. The fictive space of the novel is made manifest as a collaboratively produced graphic novel installation consisting of 165 tiles made by a cohort of 36 students, perhaps even subtly transforming the novel itself (Figure 1.2).

Stories within stories

One never remembers a story or a novel in its entirety, and never in a linear way. Therefore, we suggested that students curate "embedded narratives" from the novel, with the help of the 165 tiles created by them, based on what they could and wanted to remember. Within narrative fiction, this is termed as stories within stories, or

Figure 1.2 Graphic tiles installation (close up), various students, Avani Institute of Design.

Source: Photo by Anuradha Chatterjee.

"narratives within narratives [which] create a stratification of levels whereby each inner narrative is subordinate to the narrative within which it is embedded."[37] This does not mean just the narrative *in* the fiction, but it also refers to the "story-like representation produced in the mind of the reader," which is produced retrospectively.[38] We compared the narrative structure to a fabric and the embedded narrative as picked thread, which is "subordinate to the narrative within which it is embedded," but which contains a "segment of rationalized history" and "presents the form of a plot."[39] To this end, we asked students to select six to eight tiles (more if needed) and recompose them as a "sequence," and present them as a concertina

Figure 1.3 Embedded narratives, "Circle of Life" and "Animal Perspective,"
Azad RK, Avani Institute of Design.

(sometimes even two-sided) to convey their version of the embedded narrative. The concertina format allowed a surprising (often disruptive) number of ways to retell the same narrative. The stories that are told are not literal storylines, and the project was not intended as a meticulous inscription of the novel. The narratives that the students framed were thematic, around the issues of freedom, struggle, alienation, choice and confusion, life, death, and rebirth; homelessness and existentialist conflict – themes that pervade Mukundan's novel (Figure 1.3).

We were very keen to imagine a method of conceptualising an Interpretation Centre that was "of the place," but not in the "Framptonian" critical regionalist kind of a way. In his 1983 essay, *Towards a Critical Regionalism*, Frampton argued for architecture as a "critical practice," which sought to resist the levelling forces of placelessness of the megalopolis by evoking "the peculiarities of a particular place," through architectural inflections with respect to climate, topography, and tectonics.[40] However, as Keith L. Eggener argues, Frampton "emphasized one architect's interpretation of the region over all others," such that a "single correct regional style was implied, or imposed."[41] Other anxieties prompted by Eggener's critique were: Who was empowered to produce this sense of place, to what extent would this reflect local concern or shared meanings, what would mitigate this totalising view of place, and to what extent would critical regionalism in Mahé mean fetishising "real" place (the river) at the expense of occluding other imagined or past places? Therefore, we wanted to employ a method, whereby the idea of place was co-constructed and sustained through memories and stories of the place, through cultural and political histories that are not only partial and but also difficult to negotiate but need to be engaged with. This was referenced in and through Mukundan's *On the Banks of the Mayyazhi*. Far from allowing Mukundan's novel to provide a totalising narrative, we worked with the novel as artifice, as method, and as a point of reference.

Architectonics: Narrative and emotion

A parallel stream was that the students had also started to slowly transform the fictive and the graphic to the architectonic. This brings the conversation back to the relation between architecture and narrative. Sophia Psarra explains that narrative is a story which unfolds as a specific sequence of events, in space and time. It is structured to impart certain effects on the reader. The affinity between narrative and architecture is that both are a form of "representation bound with sequence, space and time," and like narrative, architecture "participates in construction of meaning through the ordering of spaces and social relationships."[42] What is at stake is not just the (conceptual) realm of ideas, but the way this is aligned with the (perceptual) realm of an embodied experience of visitors.[43] Psarra (through Tschumi) adds that these two realms are not "mutually exclusive," instead they are "different and interacting systems of ordering experience." Moreover, there may in fact be different kinds of narratives at play – architecture in interaction with exhibition design and artefacts; exhibition design generating its own meanings; and above all architecture, its autonomy and agency in generating narratives. Museums and galleries, argue Hale, Hurston, and McLeod, are "narrative environments," as these buildings are especially invested in storytelling and in integrating "objects and spaces" with "stories of people and places."[44] While they argue that narrative and storytelling "capture something quite fundamental about what it is to be human," they also problematise these tropes, arguing that the narrativisation involves a "process of exclusion and editing, with all the accompanying risks of bias and distortion."[45] The resolution of this is to encourage "micro-narratives" and a "'bottom-up' telling of tales," to introduce more "plurality and democracy" within this institutional space. The value of narrative is in its problematisation, such that it can be used as a provocation, "engaging the 'reader' in a creative dialogue both inspiring and revealing."

While our studio relied on narrative as a method, as a generative element, and it was less reliant on figurative representations of the narrative. Instead, it looked to Juhani Pallasmaa and Peter Zumthor's ideas of presence and atmosphere, prevailing over what Zumthor terms as the postmodernist practice of encoding architecture with messages and signs.[46] Pallasmaa defines atmosphere as a "multi-sensory fusion," and "non-material or peripheral experience," which is when one becomes aware of "immediately and without being conscious of the process."[47] Pallasmaa notes that Peter Zumthor is an atmospheric architect – an idea that is expanded in Zumthor's own book *Atmospheres: Architectural Environments: Surrounding Objects* (2006). In this book, Zumthor defines atmosphere as something we perceive "through our emotional sensibility – a form of perception that works incredibly quickly," assisted by all things environmental such as the "people, the air, noises, sound, colours, material presences, textures, forms." In buildings, these experiences (which eventually turn into lasting memories) are made possible through the physicality and mass of the building; the way materials react with each other; the aural quality of space; the temperature (physical and psychological) of materials in space; movement that similar to a cinematic assemblage of sequences encourages meandering and is "less to do with direct-ing people than seducing them," thresholds that are in a suspended state of tension between inside and outside; and the "size and mass and gravity of things" especially when they are either smaller or larger as compared to the "human scale"; and of course, the metaphysical qualities of light and the ways in which they react with materials and masses.

As each graphic tile was interpreted into an architectonic vol-ume, we reminded students to be mindful of the tendency to cre-ate abstract-gridded vector-space, and instead explore volumes that were spatialised through planes of materiality (Figure 1.4). Students thought about material effects such as lightness, heaviness, damp-ness, fragrant, resonant, reflective, dampening, fluidity, glow, incan-descence, and other experiential extremes and medians. We wanted to see if material effects could tell these stories, not figuratively, but through compelling and memorable emotional experiences. A

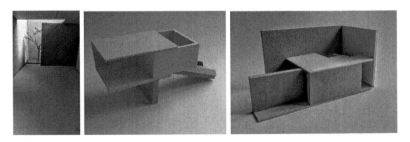

Figure 1.4 Architectonic explorations, Abhinav Sajeev C, Avani Institute of Design.

floor reflecting shadows of people walking by could evoke a certain moment in the novel; a dark and heavy ceiling could evoke feelings of feeling weighed down; and the strategic placement of a window could create a gust of wind that could evoke a certain memory. These were, at best, architectonics of approximation, which the studio was prepared to tolerate and encourage. It was interested in exploring whether the architecture of the Cultural Interpretation Centre could speak to people, to augment the narrative function of the project, in what language, to what extent, and with how much "precision." Our questions are also aligned with emerging scholarship in architecture around the notion of precision and error. Francesca Hughes's *Architecture of Error*, 2014 and, more recently, Mhairi McVicar's *Precision in Architecture*, 2019, are a timely reminder of the "pathologies behind the inflation of precision: the deployment of a degree of precision that is increasingly surplus to purpose," and that "ambiguity and deviation...are in fact critical and productive in defining architectural quality."[48]

We were interested to see the extent to which students would allow themselves to be comfortable with letting go, to allow for multivalence, ambivalence, and even ambiguity to thrive in their projects. Would they strive for strong or weak architecture? And in line with the thinking about imprecision, it was useful for us to think of this also through Ignasi de Solà-Morales's argument for "weak architecture" or architecture as "event."[49] Such architecture is "produced," but for an instant, and above all, it is an argument against monumentality, against an architecture of representation. Weak architecture, as event, finds its monumentality in recollection, not in coherence and stability of representation. The "strength of weakness" lies in architecture's willingness to accept "relegation to a secondary position," wherein it is "not aggressive and dominating, but tangential and weak."[50] Such an architecture is even termed decorative, which is that it is "inessential" and presented "not as substance." To this end, the studio anticipated that the atmospheric creations by students would be suggestive frames of being, not overpowering experiences. The methods of narrative, presence, and atmosphere were generative, and not intended as strong inscriptions.

Assemblages

The embedded narrative indicated an approximate "sequence" of event, space, and emotion, and the sequence was taken as a prompt for finding natural joints and connections between the architectonic volumes. In finding these joints, it became clear that the routes, connections, passages had to be discovered in a much more speculative manner, using a three-dimensional circulation model, moving beyond the binaries of the horizontal and vertical circulation ordained by a process driven by plans and sections. Therefore, it became possible to imagine how one might enter a volume, walk up into another, look down into yet another volume, whilst walking down and through a different volume. While the term sequence implied linearity, the articulation of it was certainly not. Students started to imagine a building as a coalesced entity, made from segments and fragments that could fit easily as well as uneasily against and into one another (Figure 1.5). One needed to imagine the process as chemically reactive, (al)chemical, such that tectonic elements slowly started to lose their identity. While the students were composing their assemblages, and the routes in and through it, they also started to consider what functional accommodation might be negotiated into these volumes, such that all key programmed spaces could be saturated to an extent with the embedded narrative.

Figure 1.5 Assemblages, first attempt, various students, Avani Institute of Design.

Source: Photo by Anuradha Chatterjee.

Lived/real city space

Another stream parallel to the reading of Mahé was the site and context study. This made the fictive space of the novel tangible, as it considered certain historical buildings and sites from the novel, such as St. Teresa's Shrine, Railway Station, Puttalam Temple, Kallappally Mosque, and the French Government Cemetery. These buildings and sites are anchor points, not just in the novel but also in the urban and cultural history of Mahé, reiterating the blurred lines between the fictive and the real. To read the urban history of Mahé in relation to its cultural history, students engaged with the different communities (based on occupation, language) looking for signs of continuities as well as disruptions in myths, legends, and stories; local produce and food; culinary traditions; language and identity; and crafts, rituals, and practices with reference to buildings and that have persisted historically. This informed the students' statement of cultural significance, which would eventually inform the programme of the Cultural Interpretation Centre.

Sited fantasies

The assemblages that students were exploring were gradually tested as sited assemblages. The project site is at the corner of Collectorate Road and another cross street, in front of Tagore Park (high historical, cultural, and social significance), and in the vicinity of important institutions like the Regional Administrator's Office. The site also has an intact historic French house, which was to be adapted and integrated into the project. The site is not only part of an important urban realm (facing Tagore Park) but it is also a politically charged one as a site of civic protests. Any design intervention would have had to consider continuity of streetscape, views to the river (beyond Tagore Park towards the Azhimukham estuary at the meeting of the river and Arabian sea), and address the adjacency to important civic buildings and public open space. Working with the assemblages on site allowed students to think of the architectonic narrative, programming and circulation, and site and urban strategy simultaneously rather than chronologically as in a conventional design process. The design thinking at this stage was one that was marked by fluidity and simultaneity. Models were assembled, arrayed, and amalgamated, as well as sited, tested, remade, and retested to arrive at a conceptual precinct plan. The three-dimensional iterations shown here revealed many possibilities for creating public as well as semi-public open spaces; articulating

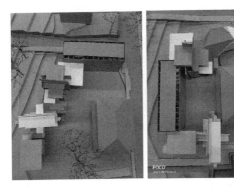

Figure 1.6 Sited assemblages, Haneena Sherin, Avani Institute of Design.

the corner; addressing the streetscape; and negotiating the new build
with the existing historic house (Figure 1.6).

Architectural becomings

The conceptual precinct plan was now scaled to 1:100 for the first
time to accommodate the architectural programme and area statement that the students had individually developed for a built-up area
of 1500 sq m. This required students to transition from the three-
dimensional, the sensorial, and the spatial to the planar, the
orthographic, and the organisational, to accommodate actual functional spaces and areas, and that too with respect to the development controls of the state, specifically setback, ground coverage and
floor area ratio (Figure 1.7). This stage was fraught with the greatest
level of anxiety, whereby the risk of abandoning difficult ideas and
lapsing into convention was highly probable. Students (as well as the
teaching team) were confronted by the kinds of volumes that had

Figure 1.7 Architectural becomings, Navaneedh Murali, Avani Institute of
        Design.

been generated, and self-imposed expectations of formal coherence, unity, and normality were palpable in many desk discussions. The non-linearity in/of the studio methodology, as discussed earlier, was not something that could be scripted, which remained emergent, and in effect invisible to us till the very end. We can now theorise that the studio was structured, not evenly, across four streams of inquiry, or "verticals," which began at different points in time in the studio chronology.

First, the novel, the graphic tiles, and the embedded narratives; second, the architectonic equivalent of each tile, the assemblages, and the modified sited assemblages; third, the site, context, and Mahé's urban and cultural history and significance, inflected through the fictive-material space of the novel; and fourth, negotiating the programme and many architectural becomings. The teaching team as well as students were weaving in and out of these verticals, so the creative methodology was neither (always) linear, nor strong. We realised how students have a way of subverting anything that is a straitjacket (framework), and we started questioning how much one should really "drive" a particular methodology. Hence, while some students had an affinity for the second vertical (architectonics), which they developed further with the help of the third and the fourth verticals (site and programme), others were inspired more by the work in the first vertical (narratives), and they appeared to bypass the architectonic stage, and go straight to the narrative, site, and programme. Others found greater safety in starting again from the third and the fourth verticals (site and programme) and finishing equally strong (Figure 1.8).

Figure 1.8 Final model, Risin CK and final model, Binciya Izara, Avani Institute of Design.

Source: Photos by Hamdan M.

As the studio travelled from fictive space of the city to the lived city; from imaging the spatial within the fiction to architectonics of emotions; from stories within stories to architectonic assemblages; from sited fantasies to many emergent architectural becomings, it concluded that no exploration is complete without methodologies of meandering. It subtly mounted an argument against this thing called "process," in favour of creative methodology (of the four parallel streams of inquiry discussed above), which enabled students to find their "home" within the broader scheme, instead of adhering to it faithfully. The studio valued method over process; navigating over arriving; and gaining insight over achieving an outcome. As we progressed through the studio, we asked ourselves: Where does one enter the project, and how does one inhabit it? Does one need to be able to control, predict the spatial effect, and to what extent? Must everything have a stable, formal representation or can this be a fleeting spatiality? What is at stake in not always knowing? What does it mean if/when the design process is embodied, physical, full of anxiety, investment? Who or what defines a successful studio project? Is it the formal resolution, or is it the operative complexities and the traces of having inhabited these complexities? And above all, what has been learnt, and what has been discovered about why and how we design, and especially the nature of collaboration?

Notes

1 Carolyn M. Shrewsbury, "What Is Feminist Pedagogy?," *Women's Studies Quarterly*, vol. 15, no. 3/4, Feminist Pedagogy (Fall–Winter, 1987): 6, 7–8.
2 Shrewsbury, "What Is Feminist Pedagogy?" 9.
3 Robbin Crabtree, David Alan Sapp, and Adela C Licona, *Feminist Pedagogy: Looking Back to Move Forward.* Baltimore (The Johns Hopkins University Press, 2009): 1.
4 Crabtree, Sapp, and Licona, *Feminist Pedagogy.*
5 Torsten Lange, Emily Scott, Lila Athanasiadou, Harriet Harriss, Andrea Merrett, Seyed Moeini, Iradj Moeini, Jane Rendell, and Sara, Rachel, "Making Trouble to Stay With: Architecture and Feminist Pedagogies," *field:*, vol. 7 (2017): 90.
6 Ibid.
7 Ibid.
8 My first exploration was the master's studio that I led at the University of New South Wales (UNSW) in 2011, which is published as Anuradha Chatterjee, "Ungraspable Criticality," in *The Routledge Companion to Criticality in Art, Architecture, and Design*, edited by Chris Brisbin and Myra Thiessen, 257–277 (Oxon, UK: Routledge, 2018). See also Aneesha Sharma and Ravi Poovaiah, "Investigation of Creative Experience

In between fiction and space   35

of Creator and Aesthetic Experience of Viewer in Design," in *Research into Design: Supporting Multiple Facets of Product Development*, edited by Amaresh Chakrabarti (Singapore: Research Publishing, 2009), 86–93.
9 David Salomon, "Experimental Cultures: On the 'End' of the Design Thesis and the Rise of the Research Studio," *Journal of Architectural Education*, vol. 65, no. 1 (2011): 42.
10 Ibid., 34.
11 Ibid.
12 Helene Furján, "Design/Research: Notes on a Manifesto," *Journal of Architectural Education*, vol. 61, no. 1 (September 2007): 61.
13 Ibid., 62.
14 Mark Wigley, "Whatever Happened to Total Design?" *Harvard Design Magazine*, no. 5 (1998). http://www.harvarddesignmagazine.org/issues/5/whatever-happened-to-total-design.
15 Chatterjee, "Ungraspable Criticality," 265.
16 Damjan Jovanovic, "Fictions: A Speculative Account of Design Mediums," in *Drawing Futures: Speculations in Contemporary Drawing for Art and Architecture*, eds. Laura Allen and Luke Caspar Pearson (London: UCL Press, 2016), 31.
17 Karl Wallick, "Tectonics Disembodied: Architectural Fragments as Generative Devices in the Studio," in *Proceedings: Tectonics 2007*, edited by Jacob Voorthuis (Eindhoven, The Netherlands: Technical University of Utrecht, 2008), 150.
18 Ibid., 152.
19 Ignasi de Solà-Morales, *Differences: Topographies of Contemporary Architecture*, edited by Sarah Whiting, translated by Graham Thompson (Cambridge: MIT Press, 1996), 23.
20 Randall Teal, "Developing a (Non-linear) Practice of Design Thinking," *The International Journal of Art & Design Education*, vol. 29, no. 3 (2010): 295.
21 Ibid., 296.
22 Giles Deleuze and Felix Guattari, *A Thousand Plateaus: Capitalism and Schizophrenia* (1987), 6–7 cited in Teal, 297.
23 Ibid., 295.
24 See Government of India, *Census of India 2011: Puducherry, District Census Handbook – Mahe*. 8. http://censusindia.gov.in/2011census/dchb/3403_PART_B_DCHB_MAHE.pdf.
25 Varkey, "The Significance of Mahe in Eighteenth-Century French India," 295.
26 See Gregory Mole, "Mahé and the Politics of Empire: Trade, Conquest, and Revolution on the Malabar Coast." *La Révolution Française*, no. 8 (2015), https://journals.openedition.org/lrf/1294; Joy Varkey, "The Significance of Mahe in Eighteenth-Century French India," *Proceedings of the Indian History Congress*, vol. 58 (1997): 295–302; District Administration Mahe, *History of Mahe*. https://mahe.gov.in/history/; and District Administration *Puducherry, History*. https://puducherry-dt.gov.in/history/.
27 Sreya Ann Oommen, "Daivathinte Vikruthikal: Homelessness and Fragmented Identities of Indo-French Families in Mahé, Post-1954," in *Anglo-Indian Identity: Past and Present, in India and the Diaspora*, edited by Robyn Andrews and Merin Simi Raj (Cham, Switzerland: Palgrave Macmillan, 2021), 374.

28 Animesh Rai, *The Legacy of French Rule in India (1674–1954): An Investigation of a Process of Creolization* (Pondichéry: Institut Français de Pondichéry, 2008), 37.
29 Oommen, "Daivathinte Vikruthikal," 385.
30 M. Mukundan, *On the Banks of the Mayyazhi*, translated by Gita Krishnankutty (Kottayam: DC Books, 2014).
31 Jayalekshmi J., "Aesthetics of Place: Exploring the Connection between Space, Time, Character and Reader in Select Malayalam Novels," *Journal of Critical Reviews*, vol. 7, no 18 (2020): 3387.
32 Swapna Gopinath, "The Dialectic of Historicity in Modernist Fiction: A Comparative Study Based on the Select Works of James Joyce, Franz Kafka, O V Vijayan, and M Mukundan" (PhD diss., University of Kerala, 2006), 262.
33 Ibid., 285.
34 Della Pollock, "Introduction: Remembering," in *Remembering: Oral History Performance*, edited by Della Pollock (New York, NY: Palgrave Macmillan, 2007, 2005).
35 Anette Arlander 1998, 58 cited in Liina Unt, "Creating the Place," in *KOHT ja PAIK / PLACE and LOCATION II Proceedings of the Estonian Academy of Arts* (Estonian Academy of Arts, 2002), 361.
36 Unt, "Creating the Place," 363.
37 Shlomith Rimmon-Kenan, *Narrative Fiction: Contemporary Poetics* (London: Methuen, 1983), 94.
38 Marie-Laure Ryan, "Embedded Narratives and Tellability," *Style*, vol. 20, no. 3 (1986), 320.
39 Rimmon-Kenan, *Narrative Fiction*, 92; Ryan "Embedded Narratives and Tellability," 323.
40 Kenneth Frampton, "Towards a Critical Regionalism," in *The Anti-Aesthetic: Essays on Postmodern Culture*, edited by Hal Foster (Port Townsend, WA: Bay Press, 1983), 21.
41 Keith L. Eggener, "Placing Resistance: A Critique of Critical Regionalism," *Journal of Architectural Education*, vol. 55, no. 4 (May 2002): 230.
42 Sophia Psarra, *Architecture and Narrative: The Formation of Space and Cultural Meaning* (Abingdon; New York, NY: Routledge, 2009), 2.
43 Ibid., 4.
44 Jonathan Hale, Suzanne Macleod, and Laura Hourston, *Museum Making: Narratives, Architectures, Exhibitions* (Abingdon, Oxon [Angleterre]; New York, NY: Routledge, 2012), xi
45 Ibid., xxi
46 See Juhani Pallasmaa, "Space, Place and Atmosphere. Emotion and Peripherical Perception in Architectural Experience," *Lebenswelt: Aesthetics and Philosophy of Experience*, no. 4 (2014): 230–245; and Peter Zumthor, *Atmospheres: Architectural Environments, Surrounding Objects* (Basel: Birkhäuser, 2006), 13, 17.
47 Juhani Pallasmaa, "Space, Place and Atmosphere. Emotion and Peripherical Perception in Architectural Experience," *Lebenswelt: Aesthetics and Philosophy of Experience*, no. 4 (2014), 230; Michael Amundsen, "Q&A with Juhani Pallasmaa on Architecture, Aesthetics of Atmospheres and the Passage of Time," *Ambiances* (2018), 2. Accessed 23 September 2020. http://journals.openedition.org/ambiances/1257.

48 Francesca Hughes, *The Architecture of Error: Matter, Measure, and the Misadventures of Precision* (Cambridge, Massachusetts: The MIT Press, 2014), 3; Mhairi McVicar, *Precision in Architectural Production: Certainty, Ambiguity and Deviation in Architectural Practice* (Milton: Routledge, 2019), 2.
49 Ignasi de Solà-Morales, "Weak Architecture," in *Differences: Topographies of Contemporary Architecture*, edited by Sarah Whiting, translated by Graham Thompson (Cambridge: MIT Press, 1996), 622.
50 Ibid., 621.

Bibliography

Amundsen, Michael. "Q&A with Juhani Pallasmaa on Architecture, Aesthetics of Atmospheres and the Passage of Time." *Ambiances*, vol. 2 (2018). Accessed 23 September 2020. http://journals.openedition.org/ambiances/1257.

Brown, Julie. "Theory or Practice—What Exactly Is Feminist Pedagogy?" *The Journal of General Education*, vol. 41 (1992): 51–63.

Chatterjee, Anuradha. "Ungraspable Criticality." In *The Routledge Companion to Criticality in Art, Architecture, and Design*, edited by Chris Brisbin and Myra Thiessen, 257–277. Oxon, UK: Routledge, 2018.

Crabtree, Robbin, David Alan Sapp, and Adela C Licona. *Feminist Pedagogy: Looking Back to Move Forward*. Baltimore, MD: The Johns Hopkins University Press, 2009.

Deloche, Jean. *Old Mahé (1721–1817): According to Eighteenth-Century French Plans*. Puducherry: Institut Français de Pondichéry and École Française d'Extrême-Orient, with Department of Art and Culture, Government of Puducherry, 2013.

District Administration Mahe. *History of Mahe*. Last Updated 15 February 2022. https://mahe.gov.in/history/.

District Administration Puducherry. *History*. Last Updated 1 February 2022. https://puducherry-dt.gov.in/history/.

Eggener, Keith L. "Placing Resistance: A Critique of Critical Regionalism." *Journal of Architectural Education*, vol. 55, no. 4 (May, 2002): 228–237.

Frampton, Kenneth. "Towards a Critical Regionalism." In *The Anti-Aesthetic: Essays on Postmodern Culture*, edited by Hal Foster, 16–30. Port Townsend, WA: Bay Press, 1983.

Furján, Helene. "Design/Research: Notes on a Manifesto." *Journal of Architectural Education*, vol. 61, no. 1 (September, 2007): 62–68.

Gopinath, Swapna. "The Dialectic of Historicity in Modernist Fiction: A Comparative Study Based on the Select Works of James Joyce, Franz Kafka, O V Vijayan, and M Mukundan." PhD diss., University of Kerala, 2006.

Government of India. *Census of India 2011: Puducherry, District Census Handbook – Mahe*. 2011. http://censusindia.gov.in/2011census/dchb/3403_PART_B_DCHB_MAHE.pdf.

Hale, Jonathan, Suzanne Macleod, and Laura Hourston. *Museum Making: Narratives, Architectures, Exhibitions*. Abingdon, Oxon [Angleterre]; New York, NY: Routledge, 2012.

Hughes, Francesca. *The Architecture of Error: Matter, Measure, and the Misadventures of Precision*. Cambridge, MA: The MIT Press, 2014.

Jayalekshmi J. "Aesthetics of Place: Exploring the Connection between Space, Time, Character and Reader in Select Malayalam Novels." *Journal of Critical Reviews*, vol. 7, no. 18 (2020): 3382–3390.

Jovanovic, Damjan. "Fictions: A Speculative Account of Design Mediums." In *Drawing Futures: Speculations in Contemporary Drawing for Art and Architecture*, edited by Laura Allen and Luke Caspar Pearson, 28–33. London: UCL Press, 2016.

Lange, Torsten, Emily Scott, Lila Athanasiadou, Harriet Harriss, Andrea Merrett, Seyed Moeini, Iradj Moeini, Jane Rendell, and Sara, Rachel. "Making Trouble to Stay With: Architecture and Feminist Pedagogies." *field:*, vol. 7 (2017): 89–99.

McVicar, Mhairi. *Precision in Architectural Production: Certainty, Ambiguity and Deviation in Architectural Practice*. Milton: Routledge, 2019.

Mole, Gregory. "Mahé and the Politics of Empire: Trade, Conquest, and Revolution on the Malabar Coast." *La Révolution Française*, no. 8 (2015). https://journals.openedition.org/lrf/1294.

Mukundan, M. *On the Banks of the Mayyazhi*. Translated by Gita Krishnankutty. Kottayam: DC Books, 2014.

Oommen, Sreya Ann. "Daivathinte Vikruthikal: Homelessness and Fragmented Identities of Indo-French Families in Mahé, Post-1954." In *Anglo-Indian identity: Past and Present, in India and the Diaspora*, edited by Robyn Andrews and Merin Simi Raj, 371–390. Cham, Switzerland: Palgrave Macmillan, 2021.

Pallasmaa, Juhani. "Space, Place and Atmosphere. Emotion and Peripherical Perception in Architectural Experience." *Lebenswelt: Aesthetics and Philosophy of Experience*, no. 4 (2014): 230–245.

Pollock, Della. "Introduction: Remembering." In *Remembering: Oral History Performance*, edited by Della Pollock, 1–18. New York, NY: Palgrave Macmillan, 2005.

Psarra, Sophia. *Architecture and Narrative: The Formation of Space and Cultural Meaning*. Abingdon; New York, NY: Routledge, 2009.

Rai, Animesh. *The Legacy of French Rule in India (1674–1954): An Investigation of a Process of Creolization*. Pondichéry: Institut Français de Pondichéry, 2008 (generated 20 September 2021). http://books.openedition.org/ifp/3369.

Rimmon-Kenan, Shlomith. *Narrative Fiction: Contemporary Poetics*. London: Methuen, 1983.

Ryan, Marie-Laure. "Embedded Narratives and Tellability." *Style*, vol. 20, no. 3 (1986): 319–340.

Salomon, David. "Experimental Cultures: On the 'End' of the Design Thesis and the Rise of the Research Studio." *Journal of Architectural Education*, vol. 65 no. 1 (2011): 33–44.

Sharma, Aneesha and Ravi Poovaiah. "Investigation of Creative Experience of Creator and Aesthetic Experience of Viewer in Design." In *Research into Design: Supporting Multiple Facets of Product Development*, edited by Amaresh Chakrabarti, 86–93. Singapore: Research Publishing, 2009.

Shrewsbury, Carolyn M. "What Is Feminist Pedagogy?," *Women's Studies Quarterly*, vol. 15, no. 3/4 (Feminist Pedagogy (Fall–Winter) (1987): 6–14.

Solà-Morales, Ignasi de. "Weak Architecture." In *Differences: Topographies of Contemporary Architecture*, edited by Sarah Whiting, translated by Graham Thompson, 616–623. Cambridge: MIT Press, 1996.

Sreelesh, VK. "The River Here: A Liquid Portrait of Mahe, India." *adda: The Online Magazine of New Writing from Around the Globe*. 20 June 2016. https://www.addastories.org/the-river-here/.

Teal, Randall. "Developing a (Non-linear) Practice of Design Thinking." *The International Journal of Art & Design Education*, vol. 29, no. 3 (2010): 294–302.

Unt, Liina. "Creating the Place." In *KOHT ja PAIK/PLACE and LOCATION II. Proceedings of the Estonian Academy of Arts*, 361–369. Tallinn, Estonia: Estonian Academy of Arts, 2002.

Varkey, Joy. "The Significance of Mahe in Eighteenth-Century French India." *Proceedings of the Indian History Congress*, vol. 58 (1997): 295–302.

Wallick, Karl. "Tectonics Disembodied: Architectural Fragments as Generative Devices in the Studio." In *Proceedings: Tectonics 2007*, edited by Jacob Voorthuis, 150–155. Eindhoven, The Netherlands: Technical University of Utrecht, 2008.

Wigley, Mark. "Whatever Happened to Total Design?" *Harvard Design Magazine*, no. 5 (1998). http://www.harvarddesignmagazine.org/issues/5/whatever-happened-to-total-design.

Zumthor, Peter. *Atmospheres: Architectural Environments. Surrounding Objects.* Basel: Birkhäuser, 2006.

2 Storytellers and outlaws

An interdisciplinary approach to teaching as research

Anca Matyiku

Introduction

Cities, landscapes, places, and spaces are multifaceted entities in which the physical manifestations of what we build is always entangled with the socio-political dynamics that are implied and taken for granted, stories that are told, and histories that are remembered. This paper reflects on the opportunities for teaching, learning, and architectural design that arise from engaging those very stories and histories. I discuss the outcome of a beginning design studio that I coordinated in the spring semester of 2020 at the University of Colorado Denver, College of Architecture and Planning. Drawing from local history on the making of the American West, students worked with the stories and histories surrounding infamous cattle robber Billy the Kid. They tackled the question of what it means to be illegal or exist on the border of the law, by writing a modern-day Billy character, and by designing a parasitic space within the urban fabric of downtown Denver. The underlying intention was to nudge students to imaginatively address delicate situations that presented themselves close at hand, in a city no stranger to gang violence and especially well acquainted with homelessness.

This interdisciplinary approach to teaching architecture is part of a broader research agenda that is invested in the cross-pollination of design with the literary imagination. While this is something I also explore in my design practice, nowhere are these questions more fruitfully asked – and tested – than in the context of design pedagogy. The claim that I pursue here with respect to storytelling and literary constructions is two-fold: that on one hand, they can capture, with more agility than drawings, the atmospheric, temporal, and multi-sensory aspects of space. On another hand, they have the capacity to engage with the complex matrix of politics, environment,

DOI: 10.4324/9781003258933-3

human motivations, and so on that underscore every act of design. Overall, this paper reiterates the importance of an interdisciplinary approach to design and design pedagogy, suggesting that a cross-pollination with the literary imagination leads to fertile opportunities towards culturally conscientious design. This emphasises an approach to design that goes beyond the formal composition of architecture and nudges students to actively consider how the formal engages and responds to this cultural horizon of an architectural project. In what follows I likewise propose that literary constructions offer an imaginatively rich variation on the concept-driven approach to design. The specific scope of this paper is to observe which literary practices proved most productive in the context of design studio.

Design as a hermeneutic dialogue: A theoretical background

Before I discuss how the literary imagination plays into design, I take a moment to present what I'm identifying as "culturally conscientious design," as an act of hermeneutics. Grounded in Hans-Georg Gadamer's philosophical hermeneutics, this understanding of design focuses on the element of interpretation and positions the *process* of design as dialectic of play conducted in earnest.[1] Interpretation through dialogue essentially means that those aspects of the design situation that are elusive and implicit – including those human values and characteristics that are socially constituted – are actively brought to speak, and play into, the design process, and thus contribute to the eventual interpretation into space-making decisions. The hermeneutic dialogue proceeds without a predetermined outcome and engages instead in a process of discovery – or an uncovering of understanding which unfolds, in a hermeneutical circle, as a perpetual "fusion of horizons" belonging to the interlocutors. In hermeneutic terms, what I earlier referred to as the "cultural horizon" refers to the context that is meaningful and specific to the design project and includes the implicit and elusive forms of knowledge that are operative in this dialogue. The architect likewise contributes their own horizon of knowledge and experience, including their biases, predispositions, and forms of knowledge that are tacit and prereflective. These many elusive, yet potent forms of knowledge play an essential role in the design process, and I will eventually argue, are very effectively captured via the literary imagination.

Educators Richard Coyne and Adrian Snodgrass have already elaborated extensively on how design thinking is grounded in a hermeneutical process.[2] They emphasise that to "define design as the manipulation of formal elements is to exclude the greater part of design."[3] Thus, with respect to design pedagogy, a hermeneutical, culturally conscientious design process cultivates an attentiveness to *how* the formal and material aspects of design are implicated in the cultural horizon that gives the design project its specificity. That design is "implicated" means that it draws on, learns from, and critically engages the cultural horizon which circumscribes the particularities of the architectural project. Coyne and Snodgrass sum up:

> We are not simply 'objects' in the world, objects without a history and as if isolated from the past, but are thrown into the midst of a network of understandings of practices, institutions, conventions, aims, tools, expectations and a multitude of other factors that make us what we are. Nor are our projections merely arbitrary productions of the subjective imagination. The projection derives from experience brought to bear on the clues scattered throughout the situation we are in. Anticipations of the completed whole are not the positing of subjectivity but emerge from pre-understandings that inhere within the situation itself.[4]

Inherent pre-understandings, along with tacit and prereflective knowledge are precisely those elusive-yet-potent forms of knowledge that are operative in design process. Tacit knowledge, as Michael Polanyi puts it, is premised on the fact that "we can know more than we can tell," and it refers to the things we know without knowing that we know them.[5] This is almost interchangeable to what phenomenology has identified as "prereflective" knowledge, that is, knowledge that evades our reflective awareness. This is the kind of embodied knowledge one acquires through experience – accrued through our bodies in engagement with the world.[6] It includes hunches and intuitions and is most easily exemplified with the expertise of a craftsperson, athlete, dancer, or musician – that is, the kind of knowledge that is difficult to explain to another person and is deployed prereflectively or tacitly rather than through conscious intent. In fact, as in the case an athlete, craftsperson, or musician, thinking about its deployment inhibits its effectiveness as it would detract from the ability to perform the task well. Polanyi points out that tacit knowledge is especially important when we are confronted with something – such as a person or a research problem – that has the capacity to surprise us because they are more complex than our conception of them. He writes that the "capacity of a thing to reveal itself in unexpected ways in the future [is attributed] to the fact that the thing observed is an aspect of a reality, possessing a significance that is not exhausted by our conception of any single aspect of it."[7] As we have noted already, design projects together with their cultural horizon are precisely such things that sustain future revelation and possess the kind of insight that overflows logic and definition.

In short, underscoring architectural design – which ultimately ends in a tangible formal and material composition – is a dialectic of active interpretation that engages forms of knowledge that are operative, but overflow our capacity to fully grasp them – both those belonging to the designer and those belonging to the project. Stated in reverse, the process by which one arrives at design involves this translation between forms of knowledge that are implicit and elusive, and the materially bounded constitution of the eventual design intervention. To engage in a dialogue with a project's extended horizon is thus to leverage the potency and wisdom of these subtle forms of knowledge that surprise us and otherwise evade the architect's initial conception.

In drawing a parallel between hermeneutics and design process, Coyne and Snodgrass outline how design process is like a dialogue that takes place in language. They insist that language, like a design project, is culturally situated and that "the language of authentic dialogue does not belong to the speakers, but rather possesses and guides them. Its function is not instrumental, but disclosive."[8] My aim is to go further and suggest that the disclosive capacity of language, especially poetic language, can in fact propel and enrich the dialectic process that underscores design. In pointing out the hermeneutics that underpin the process of design, I emphasised the delicate and nuanced (yet very active) element of interpretation. Next, I discuss how literary language can sustain and augment the element of play, towards new imaginative possibilities.

Literature and the play-element of design

Extending Gadamer's notion of play to architecture, Coyne and Snodgrass argue that like dialogue, architectural design can also be understood as a game, the rules of which are not predefined but rather circumscribed by a particular context and circumstance. For Gadamer, play is another mode through which he discusses the hermeneutic dialogue. Important to both is that the outcome is not predetermined, which means that to engage in both dialogue and play is to allow oneself to be absorbed by a process that reconfigures and reveals new understanding. Recalling Polanyi's point about engaging with problems that are more complex than our conception of them and have the capacity to surprise us, Gadamer points out that the attraction and fascination of play rests in the fact that the experience of playing overpowers the players "appearing to do surprising things of its own accord."[9] Play is thus transformative, solicits our improvisation, and opens up new insights.[10]

Gadamer's notion of play draws on Johan Huizinga's understanding that play is essential to culture-making, and in fact, intrinsically tied with poetry. "Poetry, in its original culture-making capacity, is born in and as play," Huizinga writes.[11] Furthermore, poetry which arises in play, constitutes an elemental function of the human imagination and culture: "the creative function we call poetry is rooted in a function even more primordial than culture itself, namely play."[12] To further understand how it is that poetry can operate as a form of play that reconfigures our way of seeing and being in the world, I turn to Paul Ricoeur's studies on the linguistic imagination.[13]

In his often-quoted essay "The Function of Fiction in Shaping Reality," Ricoeur makes the case that fiction suspends reality, disrupts what we take for granted as given, and in doing so it prompts us to construct new possibilities for seeing, and subsequently, new possibilities of being and acting in the world.[14] By "fiction" and "fictive" entities, Ricoeur not only means poetry, literature, and other linguistic constructions, but he also means more generally any forms of poetic representation that have the capacity to reconfigure our way of seeing – such as painting, for instance. Ricoeur does however insist that the creative imagination is fundamentally linguistic, meaning that our ability to project alternative possibilities for seeing, relies on language.[15] For Ricoeur, it is always through language that we are able to form the "image" in the mind's eye, to imagine reality otherwise, and to project other possible futures.[16] It is thus not a stretch to claim that architectural design can be understood as an act of fiction: it is a projection of potential future realities that look to creatively reconfigure the built environment.

The argument that I have been pursuing is that not only is design akin to a fictive projection into the future, but also that literature and literary constructions can in fact take part in, and fruitfully propel the design process. I noted that literary constructions are especially effective in conveying aspects of places, spaces, and cultures that are nuanced and evade definition. I here return to my two-fold claim and reiterate two modes in which this agility of the literary imagination is important to architectural design: the first is that literary constructions are especially deft in capturing atmospheric, ephemeral, temporal, and multi-sensory experiences of a place.[17] The second refers back to literature's participation to a cultural imaginary and its elemental capacity to speak to human predicaments that are ambiguous and at times contradictory. In what follows I examine how these two modes have played into design pedagogy. In the design studio discussed here, the literary imagination was engaged in the studio sequence through existing works of literature and creative texts that students wrote.

"The mind like that of a robber" – A studio premise

The student work was carried out in the context of a beginning design studio, which means that this was the students' first full-fledged design studio.[18] The project sequence covered the rudiments of beginning design which then became layered with local history. This was through the specific lens of Billy the Kid, whose short and incendiary life has achieved a kind of legendary or even mythic status in the history of the making of the American West. Billy the Kid (1859–1881) was likely born Henry McCarty and was known by a number of other pseudonyms including William H. Bonney. He was an infamously fearless cattle robber and was notorious for his swift and unflinching gunmanship. He fought in New Mexico's Lincoln County War and was charged with three murders he allegedly committed during this time. Billy the Kid was eventually shot and killed at the age of 21 by Sheriff Pat Garrett who used to be Billy's friend and accomplice. In other words, during the making of the American West, the law itself was in the making and volatile, such that Pat Garrett the robber became sheriff, the outlaw became the law. As such, the facts of history remain as tenuous as those of justice and wrongdoings, and Billy the Kid's life lent itself to romanticised variations and exaggerations. It is telling that Pat Garrett himself was compelled to write a version of Billy the Kid's biography.[19]

In the context of design studio, the character of Billy the Kid operated as a fertile opportunity for an interdisciplinary approach to teaching design. Aaron Copland's music composition for ballet "Billy the Kid," and especially Michael Ondaatje's fictional auto-biography, provided rich fodder for imaginative play.[20] The studio sequence started with students reading Ondaatje's text while engaged in a first study in drawing and composition. Here students were presented with the provocation to think like a robber – that is, to think of their drawings as a revealing that conceals, and to hunt the objects they were drawing for two-dimensional compositions.[21]

The prompt was presented through architect Carlo Scarpa who wrote that "in thinking, acting, and making [it] is necessary to have a double mind, a triple mind, the mind like that of a robber, a man who speculates, who would like to rob a bank, and it is necessary to have that which I call wit, an attentive tension toward understanding all that is happening."[22] Scarpa was lamenting a small oversight in his famous top-corner window detail at the plaster-cast museum (the Museo Antonio Canova) in Possagno, Italy. To think like a robber, in this context, meant to pay close attention to the temporally conditioned qualities such as the movement of the sun, the quality of light, the abundance of rain, fog, and so on. Students were likewise encouraged to explore in their drawings that concealed the temporal dimension of their objects as well as a variety of lighting conditions, as these would come to be part of a more explicit prompt in a subsequent step in the studio sequence.

After this initial warm-up exercise, the studio became fully immersed in the various interpretations of the Billy the Kid stories. The first step was a full-bodied drawing of Aaron Copland's ballet "Billy the Kid." From this intuitive and gestural experience in translation, students extracted a series of two-dimensional compositions, followed by a three-dimensional sequence consisting of three volumes. All of these exercises guided students through the rudiments of beginning design such that all of their compositions were articulated in response to the Billy the Kid content, meaning that their explorations in form and composition drew on the specificities of this layered cultural horizon. As the studio progressed, Michael Ondaatje's *The Collected Works of Billy the Kid* became the primary underlying force in the students' projects. Ondaatje's text is a thoughtful creative interpretation of Billy the Kid's life story. Built on historical fragments and testimonies, the text moves between poetry, prose, and reproductions of historical and archival fragments. I chose the text because it has architectural immediacy: it presents a beautifully crafted narrative that inhabits the visceral experience of what life would have been like for Billy, moving through the unforgiving, violent, and sun-drenched landscapes of the Wild West:

> The street of the slow moving animals
> while the sun drops in perfect verticals
> no wider than boots
> The dogs sleep their dreams off
> they are everywhere
> so that horses on the crowded weekend

will step back and snap a leg
[...]
The acute nerves spark
on the periphery of our bodies
while the block trunk of us
blunders as if we were
those sun drugged horses[23]

Ondaatje's fictional autobiography is crafted such that it also disrupts idealised and romanticised ideas about the Wild West. His text portrays the raw power of the landscape that is both merciless and beautiful. It also captures a nuanced picture of the complicated motivations and actions that unfolded between history, politics, and its human players.

With Ondaatje's text as an anchor, students moved from articulating their volume sequence as a sequence of three voids, that were cast into a plaster cube. This prompt is a typical one in foundations studios, and it covers the rudiments of beginning design by bringing students to understand the difference between volume and space. Students were further guided to approach the prompt by also engaging the history surrounding Billy and Ondaatje's literary text. A second iteration of the exercise prompted students to orchestrate, with care and intention, the melting of an ice-cube within this sequence of voids (Figure 2.1). This meant that they had to once again practice the attentiveness like that of a robber, and to explicitly consider temporal aspects of their design, as well as the qualitative experiences that included sound, texture, moisture, and temperature.

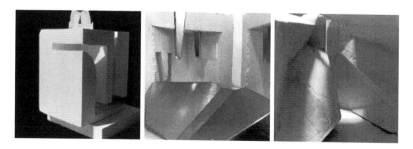

Figure 2.1 Student work: exploration of volume and void based on the Billy the Kid history and literature.

Source: From left to right Zachary Huff, Caleb Myrick, Emily Smith.

The ice-cube melt sequence was a preamble to their final project which asked students to design a parasitic hideout space that engaged the temporal and qualitatively rich cycle of snow-melt specific to Denver. During Denver's winter – which is when this studio took place – snow falls abundantly and in shorter spurts. Then, with the profuse Colorado sun, it melts quite quickly. Much of the drainage in downtown Denver is directed towards the alleyways with their variegated material palette of metal, concrete, asphalt, and brick, which altogether renders these snow-melts into veritable melodic events. For this reason, the site for the project was in a downtown Denver alleyway, behind the historic Oxford Hotel and nearby Union Station. This hideout space, that also engaged the temporalities of melting snow, was then the culminating project for this studio.

The hideout was to be designed for a modern-day Billy character, or someone who operated on the border of the law. Students were prompted to bring this character to life through a creative text. This then was the point in the studio sequence when students were not only working with existing literature but were also asked to compose their own literary texts as part of their imaginative process. Before I discuss the student's final projects, I make a brief detour to draw a parallel between a concept-based approach to design, and the literary-imagination-approach that I discuss here.

Storytelling overflows the concept

Storytelling is an act of resilience and optimism, and it is the most elemental way in which humans make sense of their world. We tell stories not only to explain certain circumstances, but, as Hans Blumenberg points out, storytelling is especially necessary to dispel the unease and uncertainty in circumstances in which answers are not possible.[24] Storytelling and the literary imagination are especially deft at capturing human situations, questions, and predicaments that are difficult, ambiguous, and contradictory. I am here recalling the complex multifaceted nuances that underscore cultures and communities which inadvertently come to bear on the built environment, and thus, I argue, can be fertile towards a design process that leads to thoughtful or culturally conscientious architecture. At stake here are forms of knowledge that speak to human concerns, yet are subtle, nuanced, and not reducible to definite, categorical, or incontrovertible truths. In short literary constructs capture human questions and predicaments without insisting on a resolution but by keeping open those questions. This, I argue, is what makes storytelling and the literary imagination especially salient for architectural design.

In prompting students to imagine a character on the border of the law, they were asked to explicitly engage with this very human, socially and politically constituted aspect of architecture. Whereas most design studio projects proceed by responding to the programme and site through a conceptual approach, in the Billy the Kid studio, students were first prompted to write a creative text about their modern-day Billy character, as they imagined them. Thus, rather than articulating a design concept for a generic person that "existed on the border of the law" they were asked to develop the particulars of their life and their predicament. My aim with this prompt was that students would first build a world on which they might later draw towards their design intervention. In comparison to a story, the concept remains in the realm of the abstract idea which can, and often does, land students on a daunting blank slate as to how to move forward with a formal and material design. It isn't that working with a literary text excludes the concept, but rather the opposite. The concept, or the design question, emerges through the story. The story has the potential to operate as a generative form of play that also uncovers new imaginative possibilities for action.[25] Thus, the architectural focus, or concept, comes immersed in the world of the story which can then become suggestive of potential architectural experiences and the spaces that might sustain them.

In his work on Giambattista Vico's *New Science* – which attributes a crucial role to the poetic imagination in the making of human knowledge – Donald Phillip Verene likewise compares the concept with the narrative. He writes that the "narrative allows us to preserve opposition which we are otherwise in danger of losing to the flatness of the concept."[26] He goes on to note that "The logic of imagination does not differ from the logic of the concept because it uses different categories but because it uses no categories at all."[27] "Categorical thought has no place for memory and the narrative. The category invites us to create ultimate singles, unequivocal grounds for thought and being. Memory and imagination allow us to treat opposition as a dramatic force."[28] Thus, one important difference between the concept and the story is that the concept tends towards resolution while the story keeps open the nuanced questions that also come to bear on the task of architecture. In storytelling, the ambivalent and contradictory forces that underscore human experience are brought forth, without demanding resolution. This means that in architecture, the story can lead to projects that sustain a multifaceted conversation about the things we build and how these built things participate in culture-making forces. The second important opportunity that the story sustains for architectural design is that it engages both memory and imagination such that, as Verene has noted, it has the potential to be leveraged as a dramatic force. I argue that this "dramatic force" is the capacity of literary constructs to propel creative action in architectural projects. To articulate this with respect to play, literary constructions not only are a form of play, but also they have the capacity to sustain a playful open-ended dialogue as the imaginative design process unfolds.[29] What kind of "literary construction" does however matter, and this is where the student projects have been especially revealing.

If I reflect on the comparison between a concept-based approach to the design studio and one that drew specifically on literary texts, I can say that in their intermediary project – the sequence of voids in which the melting of the ice-cube was orchestrated – students articulated a concept in relation to the history and literature surrounding Billy the Kid. Most students articulated a concept in their approach while also connecting qualitative aspects of the spaces they had created with those presented in the literary artefacts. When it came to the final project – which was also when students wrote their own creative texts – the students' trajectories were much more heterogeneous. In what follows I observe a few of these trajectories that were traced out by students in relation to the literary text they themselves wrote. Ultimately, I'm looking to understand if a specific kind of approaches for composing their own creative text might prove more fertile than others, when oriented towards an architectural design process.

Literary compositions for a modern-day-Billy's hideout

In my directive for the creative text that would articulate each student's modern-day interpretation of the Billy character, I emphasised that student's focus on the specific rather than the general, on qualitative details rather than a potential plot. I steered them away from describing the character. I also nudged them away from describing spaces as they might be drawn, in order to further extend the element of play, and to leverage that particular efficacy of literary language to capture aspects of human life that evade visual mediums of representation. I also asked students to focus on experiences and events – not the "who" or "what" of things, but rather what these "do" – and to describe them with as much fastidiousness and qualitative detail as possible. In other words, I wanted students to rely on the capacity of literary language to capture those temporal, ephemeral, and multi-sensory qualities of space, as well as the kinds of actions and experiences they felt captured their character – but to delay making formal decisions with respect to their design intervention. This again was a beginning design studio, and the character texts that students wrote followed this prompt with varying degrees of effectiveness.[30]

For his first text, Caleb Myrick composed a letter that he imagined Pat Garrett might have sent to Billy. The letter had a parental tone in which Garrett preached to Billy about moral uprightness. This text was quickly abandoned, and, in its place, a new narrative emerged. Caleb drew some inspiration from a comic book hero and imagined the outlaw as a righteous but deluded vigilante. The outlaw's hideout consisted of a space that amplified his voice when he decided to grace the city with his pontificating speeches. The path to the hideout was a splintered maze-like structure arranged vertically. This structure was a treacherous passage meant to obfuscate the path for anyone but the vigilante, and, mirroring his exaggerated persona, it adopted an ostentatious architectural language (Figure 2.2). For Caleb, it was telling that his initial text – which focused on moral ideologies and thus operated in the abstract – didn't do much to inspire the design process. In being more specific about rituals and qualities, the second text proved much more productive. Observed from my perspective as an instructor, it seems to me that Caleb's text didn't exactly lead him to the architecture but that the two were developed in tandem and played off each other along the way.

A similar conclusion might be drawn from Kara Admire's design process – that the design and narrative were developed together – although Kara's initial approach was quite a bit different. Her first text built onto the concept she developed in the intermediary

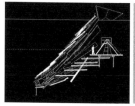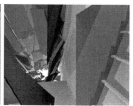

Figure 2.2 Student work: final project by Caleb Myrick.
Source: Caleb Myrick.

Figure 2.3 Student work: final project by Kara Admire.

Source: Kara Admire.

project when designing the sequence of voids. Kara was interested in the question of whether it is character or circumstance that brings a person to lawlessness. In her first text, she became preoccupied with how an innocent bystander might encounter a Billy-like character and become unwittingly embroiled in illegal acts. I would qualify this interest as being closer to a concept rather than a creative text. In other words, the architectural implications of this question, although poignant, were missing the specifics of qualitative experience. Part of Kara's process was to figure out how specifically this interest might manifest itself as a hideout for such a person. In stark contrast to Caleb's design approach, Kara became interested in a discreet, clandestine hideout that re-appropriated the existing infrastructure of rooftop HVAC (heating, ventilation, and air conditioning) units (Figure 2.3). This gesture became the driver for her specific narrative, which was not in fact officially put into written text until the design of the space was near its end. The new narrative revealed the circumstance that brought this character to homelessness and how they came to find a hideout space in a defunct rooftop HVAC unit.

For Antonio Luna, the creative text exercise did not become a significant driver in his hideout design. Antonio imagined his character as a parkour artist and designed an escape sequence through a low-level water drain under the alley, and up an elaborate sculptural structure that was meant to obfuscate Billy's escape through reflections and glare (Figure 2.4). This structure played with the sun – which in Colorado is known to be present for 300 days of the year – to articulate a game of appearance and disappearance. The stronger driver for Antonio was a conceptual image of a crystal refracting light that he brought to the table. His own text was developed together with the design and echoed the same superhuman agility and free-spirited detachment he read in the historical Billy the Kid. In other words, the stories and literature surrounding Billy the Kid that I had provided,

Figure 2.4 Student work: final project by Antonio Luna-Rincon.

Source: Antonio Luna-Rincon.

seemed to have had a stronger impact for Antonio than the creative text he himself wrote.

Another student, Emily Smith, was likewise interested in engaging the sun but for her this interest came from the Ondaatje text, to which she maintained a close connection for the hideout project. Emily collected the passages in which Ondaatje attentively conveys the presence of the sun, capturing a richly nuanced relationship between Billy's life and the landscape of the Wild West. There are instances in which the sun's unforgiving indifference reiterates the cruelty of the Wild West. Through Ondaatje's voice, Billy tells us how:

> Charlie lying dead on the horse's back, [...] A sheet covered him to stop him from drying too much in the sun.[31]
>
> The sun sat back and watched while the juice evaporated. By now the bone was dull white, all dry.[32]

The sun is also how Ondaatje, in other passages, articulates an edge condition, the tension that would have been lurking around every corner of Billy's life:

> I am here on the edge of sun
> that would ignite me
> looking out into pitch white
> sky and grass overdeveloped to meaninglessness

waiting for enemies' friends or mine.[33]
I am 4 feet inside the room
in the brown cold dark
the doorway's slide of sun
three inches from my shoes
I am on the edge of the cold dark[34]

Finally, Emily noticed how Ondaatje's sun also recasts space in a comforting angelic luminescence that stands in stark contrast to the bloody violence of the Wild West:

> About 9 o'clock and the room looks huge like the sun came in and pushed out the walls, the sun – as it reflected off the bushes outside - swirling on the white walls and the white sheets on the bed as I can see when I put my head up.[35]
> It is afternoon still, the room white with light. My last white room, the sun coming down through the shutters making the white walls wither. I lie on my left cheek looking at that light.[36]

Emily became invested in the condition of the edge – of the shadow, and the point of sharp contrast. She looked to inhabit this edge, and to give it a depth, to create shadows inside shadows. She carefully studied the shadows that were cast in the alley and built the hideout inside the shadows (Figure 2.5). In her design process, one

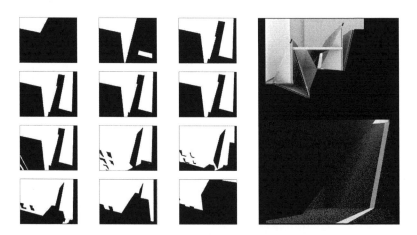

Figure 2.5 Student work: shadow studies and final project by Emily Smith.
Source: Emily Smith.

notices obsessive interest in measure that is accompanied by a poetic response to the site and the Colorado sun – both of which are qualities that also came forth in Ondaatje's text. I found this approach to the project to be especially sophisticated for a beginning design student, even if it did make the final project more difficult to resolve in the allotted timeframe.

Reflections

Overall, the students' own creative texts proved to be less of a driving force in the design of their hideouts than I had anticipated. I still however believe it be an important accompaniment to the process of design, and the teaching of design. Often enough there are students who produce astounding texts, and when this happens it is immensely rewarding. What matters more is that they write it. All creative texts have the potential to help students find a focus to their project. If we revisit the earlier parallel to a concept-based approach to design, we could say that the concept for all the students boiled down to "hiding in plain sight" – whether in a discreet or ostentatious manner. The "how" of what that meant, materially and architecturally, gained specificity from the stories and characters they wrote. In addition, the students' texts reinforced my belief that most productive towards design were those literary texts that focused on specific qualitative, temporal, and experiential conditions and not texts that offered more general or abstract ideas and insights. What I discovered with Kara and Caleb was that composing such a text is by no means an easy task and can in fact prove to be as much of a design problem as the architecture itself. With Emily I noticed that staying close to the text written by a professional author was in fact more fruitful. Finally, with Antonio I discovered that a creative text can reinforce design intentions but that perhaps still more compelling was again, the engagement with the thoughtfully crafted stories and literature of an author.

My goal with this project was to present students – right from their first design studio – with the notion that architectural design is not just a form-finding exercise but is part of a multifaceted matrix of forces that includes politics, social values, and norms, along with human ambitions, motivations, and circumstance. In working with the stories and cultural artefacts surrounding Billy the Kid, students were able to grasp that often polarised ideas about moral righteousness or social justice are in fact often contradictory, nuanced, and delicate. Many of them were able to poignantly engage these nuanced and delicate human predicaments in their architectural designs. This, I am convinced, would not have been possible – not at the same level of sophistication – if students were only presented with the conceptual prompt of designing a space for a person who existed on the border of the law. The story of Billy the Kid, Ondaatje's fictional autobiography and yes, the students' creative texts, situated this architectural question in specificity. What I learned with Studio Billy the Kid was that the voice of a professional writer is essential to capturing this potent aspect of storytelling. Ultimately, it was the stories surrounding Billy, articulated through Ondaatje's text, that most saliently carried the student's engagement with the prompt. I chose the text because of its architectural import – especially articulated in the way it was invested in the qualitative and experiential elements of the landscape of the Wild West. In other words, the choice of literary text can be seen as a crucial design decision – which in this instance was a design decision on the side of the instructor.

In reflecting on the Billy the Kid studio, I have learned that presenting students with compelling literary works is important towards engaging them to consider the full complexity of architecture's participation to human concerns. Prompting students to compose their own literary texts gives them the opportunity to tease out their architectural interests via multiple mediums of expression. Even if the texts they write do not become explicit in their final studio project, what becomes important in this process is that students bring their voice to the project. To ask students to imagine another human and tell their story is in effect to ask them to invest the project with something about which they care. This nudges them to trust their tacit knowledge and to engage their life experiences in their own design practice and towards culturally conscientious design. I insist that this act of interpretation across mediums that calls on subtle yet multi-layered forms of knowledge is crucial to building one's creative imagination and it does in fact require practice, discipline, as well as playfulness.

Notes

1 I will be referring primarily to Gadamer most significant work on philosophical hermeneutics, Hans-Georg Gadamer, *Truth and Method,* trans. Joel Weinsheimer and Donald G. Marshall (London, New Delhi, New York, Sidney: Bloomsbury Academic, 2013).
2 For their extensive parallel between hermeneutics and design process, see "Chapter 1: Architectural Hermeneutics" in Richard Coyne and Adrian Snodgrass, *Interpretation in Architecture: Design as a Way of Thinking* (London: Routledge, 2005).

3 Ibid., 55.
4 Ibid., 39.
5 Michael Polanyi, *The Tacit Dimension* (Chicago and London: University of Chicago Press, 1966), 4.
6 Tacit or prereflective knowledge is not "unconscious" as understood by psychoanalysis because it is not repressed. It is likewise not "subjective" knowledge. In fact, the aim of hermeneutics is to reveal the objective-subjective dichotomy as ineffectual with respect to the humanities. Hermeneutics insists that there is not such a thing as an objectively valid interpretation because it is always situated, that is, always operates within a horizon of understanding. In fact, what we understand as objective categories are nothing other than the result of interpretive preconceptions.
7 Polanyi, *The Tacit Dimension*, 32.
8 Coyne and Snodgrass, 49.
9 Gadamer, *Truth and Method*, 110.
10 While hermeneutics has its basis in the interpretation of historical texts, Gadamer's goal is to show that through the hermeneutic dialogue and play, all works, including painting, sculpture, and theatre, are not simply objects to be beheld but operate within a world (their horizon) and have the capacity to renew (self) understanding.
11 Johan Huizinga, *Homo Ludens: A Study of the Play Element in Culture* (Boston: Beacon Press, 1955), 122.
12 Ibid., 132.
13 Scholarship that discusses the operative capacity of metaphoric language for architectural design often relies on Paul Ricoeur's studies on the linguistic imagination. For instance, Klaske Havik, *Urban Literacy: Reading and Writing Architecture* (Rotterdam: nai010 Publishers, 2014).
14 Paul Ricoeur, "The Function of Fiction in Shaping Reality," *Man and World* 12, no. 2 (1979): 123–141.
15 Ricoeur develops this most extensively through the notion of metaphor, in Paul Ricoeur, *The Rule of Metaphor: Multi-Disciplinary Studies of the Creation of Meaning in Language*, trans. Robert Czerny (Toronto, Buffalo, London: University of Toronto Press, 2000).
16 We might transfer Ricoeur's argument to architecture to say that when we imagine a space that we have never before experienced – such as a deep dark well filled with dancing fireflies punctuated by the intermittent echo of dripping water – we in fact, first and foremost, rely on language to construct this not-yet-existing image.
17 I have also previously made the case that literary representations can capture atmospheric and multi-sensory qualities of a space with more agility than visual modes of representation. Anca Matyiku, "Architecture Drawn Out of Bruno Schulz's Poetic Prose," in *Reading Architecture: Literary Imagination and Architectural Experience*, eds. A. Sioli and Y. Jung. (New York, London: Routledge, 2018). Anca Matyiku, "Literary Language and Palimpsests of Chronometries: Representations of Urban Space in Bruno Schulz's Prose," in *La Città Palinsesto / The City as Palimpsest*, ed. Maria Ines Pascariello (Napoli: FedOA – Federico II University Press, 2020).
18 The student work was carried out in the context of a beginning design studio with a cohort of around 48 students. I was the studio coordinator

which meant that I designed the project sequence and fine-tuned it together with three colleagues. The studio sequence would not have been what it was without the fantastic conversations and tremendous insights of my colleagues Michelle Frankel, Brian Dale, and Paul Mitchell. I am indebted to them and very grateful for the opportunity to have worked together on this studio sequence. I am also indebted to all the students with whom I had the fortune to work in my studio section, and especially to Zachary Huff, Kara Admire, Antonio Luna-Rincon, Caleb Myrick, and Emily Smith who have granted their permission to include their work here.

19 Pat F. Garrett, *The Authentic Life of Billy, the Kid: The Noted Desperado of the Southwest, Whose Deeds of Daring and Blood Made His Name a Terror in New Mexico, Arizona and Northern Mexico* (Houston: Frontier Press of Texas, 1953).

20 There is also Sam Peckinpah's 1973 film (staring and with a soundtrack by Bob Dylan), which contributed to the constellation of cultural artefacts surrounding Billy the Kid. While students were made aware of this film we did not explicitly engage it in the studio sequence.

21 Michael Ondaatje, *The Collected Works of Billy the Kid,* 2nd ed (New York: Vintage International, 2009).

22 Carlo Scarpa, Scarpa, Carlo. "Volevo ritagliare l'azzuro del cielo," *Rassegna 7 (Carlo Scarpa, Frammenti 1926/1978)* (1981): 83–84. (translation with my adjustments).

23 Ondaatje, *The Collected Works of Billy the Kid, 75.*

24 Blumenberg's is a study on myth, specifically looking at how myths persist over time and repeat in new variations according to their particular circumstance. Hans Blumenberg, *Work on Myth,* trans. Robert M. Wallace (Cambridge, MA: MIT Press, 1985). See Part I Ch. 4: "Procedural Regulations," especially 126–128.

25 I also explored a version of this argument in the context of fabrication courses: Anca Matyiku, "Project Daedalus: An Earnest Play of Building Between Storytelling and Metaphors," *Writingplace Journal: Literary Methods in Architectural Education,* no. 1 (2018): 59–74.

26 Donald Phillip Verene, *Vico's Science of Imagination* (Ithaca and London: Cornell University Press, 1981): 191–192.

27 Ibid., 217.

28 Ibid., 216.

29 A more demonstrative version of this argument can be found in Matyiku, "Architecture Drawn Out of Schulz's Prose." Here I examine the playful, synesthetically rich, exaggerated metaphors in the architectural images of Bruno Schulz's prose.

30 I recognise that the design process is much messier and less straightforward than I will be presenting here. I likewise recognise that I am describing someone else's process without having direct access to their experience. As such my own biases and presumptions are inflecting my observations of how each student's process translated into their final design.

31 Ondaatje, *The Collected Works of Billy the Kid, 79.*

32 Ibid., 80.

33 Ibid., 78.

34 Ibid., 77.

35 Ibid., 71.
36 Ibid., 82.

Bibliography

Blumenberg, Hans. *Work on Myth.* Translated by Robert M. Wallace. Cambridge, MA: MIT Press, 1985.

Coyne, Richard and Adrian Snodgrass. *Interpretation in Architecture: Design as a Way of Thinking.* London: Routledge, 2005.

Gadamer, Hans-Georg. *Truth and Method.* Translated by Joel Weinsheimer and Donald G. Marshall. London, New Delhi, New York, NY, Sidney: Bloomsbury Academic, 2013.

Garrett, Pat F. *The Authentic Life of Billy, the Kid: The Noted Desperado of the Southwest, Whose Deeds of Daring and Blood Made His Name a Terror in New Mexico, Arizona and Northern Mexico.* Houston, TX: Frontier Press of Texas, 1953.

Havik, Klaske. *Urban Literacy: Reading and Writing Architecture.* Rotterdam: nai010 Publishers, 2014.

Huizinga, Johan. *Homo Ludens: A Study of the Play-Element in Culture.* Boston, MA: Beacon Press, 1955.

Matyiku, Anca. "Architecture Drawn out of Bruno Schulz's Poetic Prose." In *Reading Architecture: Literary Imagination and Architectural Experience,* edited by A. Sioli and Y. Jung, 114–122. New York, NY, London: Routledge, 2018.

Matyiku, Anca. "Project Daedalus: An Earnest Play of Building Between Storytelling and Metaphors." *Writingplace Journal: Literary Methods in Architectural Education* 1 (2018): 59–74.

Matyiku, Anca. "Literary Language and Palimpsests of Chronometries: Representations of Urban Space in Bruno Schulz's Prose." In *La Città Palinsesto/The City as Palimpsest,* edited by Maria Ines Pascariello, 365–370. Napoli: FedOA – Federico II University Press, 2020. http://www.fedoabooks.unina.it/index.php/fedoapress/catalog/view/249/279/1464-1.

Ondaatje, Michael. *The Collected Works of Billy the Kid.* 2nd ed. New York, NY: Vintage International, 2009.

Polanyi, Michael. *The Tacit Dimension.* Chicago and London: University of Chicago Press, 1966.

Ricoeur, Paul. "The Function of Fiction in Shaping Reality." *Man and World* 12, no. 2 (1979): 123–141.

Ricoeur, Paul. *The Rule of Metaphor: Multi-Disciplinary Studies of the Creation of Meaning in Language.* Translated by Robert Czerny. Toronto, Buffalo, London: University of Toronto Press, 2000.

Scarpa, Carlo. "Volevo ritagliare l'azzuro del cielo." *Rassegna 7 (Carlo Scarpa, Frammenti 1926/1978)* (1981): 82–85.

Verene, Donald Phillip. *Vico's Science of Imagination.* Ithaca, NY and London: Cornell University Press, 1981.

3 On literature and architecture

Imaginative representations
of space

Angeliki Sioli and Kristen Kelsch

Introduction

When architecture students engage in the act of design, what acti-
vates their imagination and positions them to work in a way that
welcomes spatial and representational experimentation? In which
ways can students pull forward original and imaginative modes of
space-perception, depiction, and design? How can disciplines, not
traditionally associated with architecture, serve as a strong context
in exercising architectural imagination for drawing new and unique
spatial conditions? Such questions may be addressed by exploring
research on the intersection of architecture, literature, and imagination, and the ways an interdisciplinary approach may influence design studio pedagogy. The educational approach examined
emerges from a theoretical framework studying how imagination
works. By focusing specifically on what philosopher Paul Ricoeur has
called "literary imagination"[1] the research aims to demonstrate how
literature, with its evocative descriptions, word-metaphors, and polysemic expressions, may trigger students' personal and distinctively
unique imagination, and thus cultivate their spatial thinking.

Literary imagination

By literary imagination, we mean the imaginative thinking which
springs in our brain when we are reading a novel, story, poem, or
narrative, in short, a literary piece. The spatial descriptions captured by the polysemic and metaphorical language of literature,
form imaginative representations of space in the reader's mind. The
representations are uniquely connected to the reader's own associations with the words they read and absorb. In her work *Dreaming
by the Book* (2001), Elaine Scarry explains that literary descriptions

DOI: 10.4324/9781003258933-4

of spaces are more vivacious and meaningful than pictorial images, because they depend on the active and intimate involvement of a reader's own imagination.[2] Pictorial images of space, on the contrary, presuppose a more passive attitude, since the reader/observer does not author them, but rather consumes them.[3] We suspect that, to a certain degree, such consumption can hinder imaginative and critical engagement with space when it comes to architectural education. To bypass such a predicament, we argue in favour of the use of literature in the education of an architect.

Research into imagination often emphasises its connection to vision, portraying imagination as a unique way of seeing the world by forming mental images in the brain.[4] Philosophers Richard Kearney and Paul Ricoeur, however, pursue a connection between imagination and language. For example, Kearney posited that as we shift from description to interpretation, as we interpret the linguistic descriptions that we process through reading, imagination is considered more in terms of language.[5] Similarly, Ricoeur points to the fact that the creation of new meanings in language is strongly linked to imagination. He explains that imagination, while it can be highly productive in creating multiple possible images, it first and foremost has linguistic origins. The emergence of new meanings through language can lead to the innovative creation of new images, images inherently connected with cultural values just like language itself.[6] Ricoeur places a great importance on the role of metaphors in languages for the creation of new linguistic meanings and subsequently new images. Following Aristotle's thinking, he looks at metaphors as this wondrous capacity of language to reveal similarities among seemingly dissimilar ideas, concepts, and fields.[7] For Ricoeur, imagination is precisely this capacity to connect opposing meanings, creating an unprecedented semantic pertinence from an old semantic impertinence.[8] Recently, such observations have been corroborated with findings from the field of neuroscience. In his work *The Architect's Brain* (2011) scholar Harry Mallgrave, discussing experiments run by the renowned neurologist V.S. Ramachandran, identifies that what artists, poets, and novelists all have in common, is their skill at forming metaphors, linking seemingly unrelated concepts in their brain.[9]

From the discipline of architecture also more and more voices seem to argue in favour of language and literary imagination for education. Theoretician Alberto Pérez-Gómez discusses architectural representation in relation to literary imagination, by arguing that "literary narratives can contribute greatly to the design of programs for future living, woven from significant actions, configuring thus properly attuned atmospheres" in place.[10] Additionally, educator and practitioner Anca Matyiku explores the use of literary images and linguistic metaphors for architectural design in her article "Architecture Drawn Out of Bruno Schulz's Poetic Prose" (2018). She posits "that literature operates in tandem with drawing, as an instrument for architectural design," and that "literary texts [should] be used toward *and* together with drawing in the process of finding the future architecture."[11] Educators Lisa Landrum and Klaske Havik come to literature's support as well. Landrum stresses the importance of linguistic and literary imagination for students arguing that "when we describe the 'ceiling; of a room as its overarching 'sky,' we begin to lift and open that ceiling to a more poetic and universally resonate realm of worldly conditions," that helps the students see it anew.[12] Havik, on the other hand, investigates how literary techniques – employed by authors and poets – can be of use in architectural education. By doing so, she brings to our attention that "in literature the experiences of space and spatial practices are often much more accurately described than in professional writings on architecture and cities, whether in the form of architectural history, criticism or design theory."[13]

With such philosophical, scientific, and architectural underpinnings working as the foundation of our research and teaching pedagogy, we set out to explore how literary language might lead students' imagination to author original spatial understandings and become a catalyst for dreaming up, and drawing unique architectural possibilities (see Figure 3.1).

Imagining place through literature: Undergraduate work

During the beginning stages of architectural education is where we introduce experiments into the possibilities of literature and literary imagination in relation to the medium of drawing. It is in these first formative years that students spend a substantial amount of their education working to understand the rules and conventions of orthographic projection, perspectival views, and notational drawings. Though these commonly used architectural drawing techniques carry strong assumptions and ideas about space that express only specific and even limited spatial possibilities. To open students to the richness of drawing and enhance their understanding of its representational capacity to capture and convey space, we engage with literature. We connect the literary readings with bigger design assignments to come, this approach works to eliminate fears of the blank page and

Figure 3.1 Reading literary narratives out loud in an underground design studio course, Louisiana State University, 2017.

Source: Photograph by the authors.

struggles which come with starting new ideas and spatial inspirations. These literary readings are planned pauses in the fast-paced rhythm of the semester. They are a chance for students to breathe, reflect, and experiment. All students are required to produce drawings, but the outcomes are not graded. This exercise is viewed as a way to promote student exploration, and the students appear to appreciate such an open learning opportunity, as they are often run down by the usual confines of grading and constant evaluation that architectural education entails. Moreover, the environment in which these readings and related drawings unfold is controlled. Use of cell phones or laptops, search engines or precedents are not permitted, nor are any deviations from the very simple act of reading and drawing entertained.[14]

In a recent design studio course (2017) – while preparing students to design underground worlds – we set out to draw spatial conditions depicted in the novel *The Windup Bird Chronicle* (1995) by Haruki Murakami and the short story "The Burrow" (1931) by Franz Kafka.[15] Both texts describe subterranean environments and dark spaces; wells, tunnels, and burrows. In the context of the assignment, literature works as a generative tool for imaginative spatial drawings that depict these underground conditions. The students create one drawing per narrative using pencil, ink, or charcoal. They are encouraged to work on any view or conflation of views, with the understanding that they do not introduce elements foreign to the stories. The assignment brief guides the focus of their attention precisely on the spatial elements:

> Try to imagine the places described in the narrative as vividly as possible. Get specific. Envision the spatial qualities mentioned by the author, the general configuration of the main elements, the materials described, the dimensions, the time of the day or night, the light in the spaces, the atmosphere, the space-related emotions felt by the characters (a sense of enclosure, a sense of protection, a sense of being lost, etc.). Take the time to pay attention to all the elements of the inhabitable spaces described, even if they seem unconventional or paradoxical. Give your drawings a short title. Do not try to depict all the elements described by the authors. If the narrative makes you feel that some elements are more important than others, prioritise them and create your drawings accordingly. This might differ from your class-mates. Pick elements and descriptions of the places that inspire you, and motivate your imagination.[16]

In the beginning, the studio is quiet as students move from reading to sketching and from sketching back to reading. Peer-exchange and collaborations – practices highly valued during any other time – are suspended. This is an unsettling moment in the studio and it is intentional. It is for the same reason that we select descriptions of underground worlds – a spatial condition particularly unfamiliar and not overly common – so as to make sure all students feel equally uneasy with the task at hand and they rely on the literary process instead of turning to each other for guidance.

Inhabiting the well

In the evocative Murakami narrative, the main protagonist discovers and inhabits a well in the middle of busy Tokyo. Excerpts describing elements of this experience served as excellent starting points to engage students' imagination. Surprisingly enough the literary descriptions also helped some students understand what a well is. In a place like Louisiana where wells are not necessary and water

comes plentiful from the sky (through regular or even intense tropi-
cal rains) we realised that the assignment started with a confusion. A
well was mistaken for a water repository. Clarifying this unexpected
misunderstanding, allowed the students to understand the literary
descriptions properly and proceed to build drawings that fell outside
the usual drawing conventions. One excerpt focused on the steel ladder that one climbs in order to descend into the well:

> I climb down the steel ladder anchored in the side of the well (...) I
> listen hard for anything new; I take a lungful of air; (...) I check the
> hardness of the wall (...) A round slice of light floats above me (...)
> Things down here stay very still. I take several deep breaths, letting
> my body grow accustomed to this deep, dark, cylindrical space.[17]

From reading this excerpt, initial thoughts about the ladder emerge:
How long is the ladder, is it steep or old, how comfortable or safe does
it feel as someone slowly descends? What does it mean to leave behind
a luminous sunny space – "a round slice of light" that "floats above"
as the metaphor beautifully describes –and how does it feel to have
the only light come from a top opening? Those who decide to work
with descriptions referring to the descent into the well consider these
questions. Some sketch possibilities where the ladder is positioned
near the side of the paper seeking to emphasise the looming void that
awaits as somebody descends into the darkness below. Others become
fascinated by how more comfortable and at ease the protagonist feels
after completing several descents, so they experiment with a very com-
pressed configuration – one where ladder and walls are in close proximity to each other – hoping to communicate that the fear of falling
in the gap diminishes after a while. These differences in approach
spark one-on-one exchanges on how our own feelings and emotions
influence our perception and understanding of space – impacting
what we notice or fail to notice – and how our drawings of places and
architecture are subject to these influences.

Meanwhile, other students concentrate their spatial investigations
on descriptions of the well's entrance and its presence in the middle of
an abandoned city lot close to a tree.

> I leaned over the edge again and looked down into the darkness,
> anticipating nothing in particular. So, I though, in a place like
> this, in the middle of the day like this, there existed a darkness as
> deep as this. (...) I put the cover back on the well and set the block
> atop it.[18]

This description of a threshold triggers students to develop different ideas which lead to drawing the darkness in diverse ways. Some
imagine the darkness as menacing and some surprise us by thinking
of the darkness as a calm and soothing presence in the chaos of a
loud metropolis. They opt to depict it in a very evocative and positive
light. As the narrative mentions a cover, this becomes a very important architectural consideration. Students must determine how much
of this entrance should be represented, or how the cover works and to
what extent it protects the entrance to the well. Others seem to think
that inhabiting a well is a fascinating possibility and refuse to believe
the fear that the protagonist feels initially. We direct them back to the
literary descriptions and make sure that they do not impose their own
feelings or perceptions onto the way the space is experienced by the
protagonist himself.

Murakami's novel is written in a seemingly objective manner. It
avoids subjective emotional qualifications and generates an experience of attunement between environments and task, action, and habit,
which the students end up capturing with their drawings. In one-
to-one discussions with them, we help them unpack the metaphors,
descriptions, and pictorial images embedded in the narrative, without
influencing their understanding of them. These conversations allow
students to focus on their own imagination and express spatial elements of light, darkness, ascend or descend, tangible materiality or
feelings, and sensations. Ultimately, the results which emerge from the
exact same words are unique and specific to each student's interpretation of those words (see Figure 3.2).

Creating a burrow

On the other hand, the Kafka short story – which is distributed during a second session – proves to be a more challenging text, as it
describes a much larger and chaotic underground structure in an
emotionally intense manner. The author's poetic literary language
reveals an elaborate network of subterranean tunnels and rooms,
and the students dive into their own imaginations once again, trying
to depict them through the drawings.

> Every hundred yards I have widened the passages into little
> round cells; there I can curl myself up in comfort and lie warm.
> There I sleep the sweet sleep of tranquility, of satisfied desire of
> achieved ambitions... (...) There are more than fifty such rooms
> in my burrow.[19]

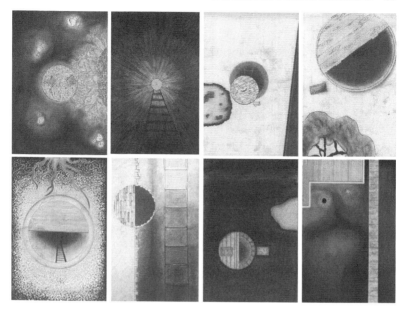

Figure 3.2 Selected students' drawings depicting different elements of the
well described in Haruki Murakami's novel The Wind-Up Bird
Chronicle, Louisiana State University, 2017.

Source: Image of Bachelor of Architecture '21 candidates' work provided by the authors.

From working with such passages multiple relevant spatial questions
arise once again. How are these small curved out rooms arranged or
formed? How do they offer a sense of comfort and security? The initial sketches vary substantially. Students who represent the burrow in
all its complexities overwhelm the paper with countless small spaces
and draw the network which unites them. For some, the passageways
themselves become a point of interest, an element warranting attention. Different perspectives are captured, as well as geometries that
work with the body of the Kafka's character. Combined views appear,
as some drawing explorations simultaneously depict the entrance to
the burrow and the deepest and darkest room described. And still yet,
other drawings use merged perspectives with plans and diagrams to
depict both how it might feel to be in the maze of tunnels while also
wanting to escape it.

By the end of the exercise, students put forward "semantic inno-
vations" or in the words of Ricoeur: "unprecedented semantic per-
tinences" for architectural and spatial conditions. The drawings

communicate stories of place that are unique to a student's personal spatial perception. Engaging with literature and drawing enriches their imagination and enables them to access new (previously unimagined) drawn possibilities. The combined views, for example, are unexpected creative outlets that address the complexities of this drawing assignment and capture the richness of the spatial descriptions. At the same time, the sketches and drawings capture shortcomings of our relationships with language. Familiar and everyday words, which carry strong personal associations, are easily misunderstood or overlooked in the course of this assignment. When Kafka describes a creature that "sniffs the air," for example, some students assume that the inhabitant of the burrow is a dog and draw canines in their depictions. In other words, oftentimes a word is so strongly related to a specific association, that their imagination will not even let them question this association. In these instances, the students are challenged to acknowledge such habits and research definitions of words or meanings of expressions before proceeding. To help them re-imagine the spatial conditions as experienced by the unidentified character that Kafka has created, drawings on trace paper are encouraged. The informal, layered material lends itself to trial and error, drawing, and redrawing, ultimately helping students overcome their hesitations in changing their drawings.

At the end of the two sessions, each student has created two unique drawings. In celebration, an exhibition of the work takes place along the walls of the school's main corridor. Students explore the work of the whole class, dive into their colleagues' imaginative worlds, exchange ideas, share confusions about the process, and discuss differences. This is the first opportunity they have to view each other's work, as their drawings were collected and stored after each session concluded.

Imagining place through literature: Graduate work

In more advanced stages of architectural education, we engage literature to challenge students' acquired certainties and habits. In some instances, students are invited to study architectural elements that are usually difficult to capture and design, such as the elusive atmospheres of place and how they can influence the design of specific artefacts. Under other circumstances, literature becomes an integral part of their design process, serving as a generative tool used to inspire and organise architectural programme and space. Similar to the undergraduate experiences, the students push through a challenging engagement with select texts and ultimately produce rich, unexpected, and revealing drawings, artefacts, and ideas.

Surviving the Red Death

At a recent graduate design studio (2018),[20] the students were charged with creating a device for the body. To do so, they immersed themselves into a particularly evocative atmospheric environment, as the one captured by Edgar Allan Poe's short story "The Masque of the Red Death" (1842). In the narrative, a prince hosts a lavish masquerade. He welcomes thousands behind his castle walls offering the guests entertainment as well as a chance to avoid the fatal plague of the Red Death. Ultimately, the threat still looms, penetrates the castle, and ends the festivities by assassinating the prince and contaminating his guests. As captured by Poe's poetic writing, an extravagant, mysterious, but also macabre, atmosphere appears to dominate the palace. The literary language depicts different examples of interaction between the physical space and the bodies of the guests. Leaning on this narrative, we explore how literary imagination can work in an assignment that calls for this very interaction between physical space and body. The literary narrative is chosen precisely because it describes an embodied interaction with space and its ephemeral atmospheric elements, opening the possibility for students to design for this very experience.

Multiple readings of the narrative and drawings capturing the depicted spatial atmospheres guide the students to imagine themselves as guests in the masquerade. They are to imagine how they might respond to the spatial conditions that the threat poses. The design assignment calls for the creation of a device that would simultaneously allow them to celebrate among the crowd and protect themselves from the imminent death. Some students imagine that their body would feel great tension and they would be completely distressed, had they attended such a masquerade, so they want to create something that allows them to maintain full visual access to the palace. Others engage with the literary descriptions in a more playful way and begin imagining how a mask may provide them both an impenetrable hiding place and premium access to the happenings of the night. The devices emerged after the meticulous and careful work with the literary piece, the evocative descriptions communicated through the language of Edgar Allan Poe. The following excerpt portrays the eccentric palace setting in which the students have to imagine themselves:

> There were much of the beautiful, much of the wanton, much of the bizarre, something of the terrible, and not a little of that which might have excited disgust. To and fro in the seven chambers there stalked, in fact, a multitude of dreams. And these – the dreams – writhed in and about, taking hue from the rooms, and causing the wild music of the orchestra to seem as the echo of their steps. And, anon, there strikes the ebony clock which stands in the hall of the velvet. And then, for a moment, all is still, and all is silent save the voice of the clock. The dreams are stiff-frozen as they stand. But the echoes of the chime die away – they have endured but an instant – and a light, half-subdued laughter floats after them as they depart. And now again the music swells, and the dreams live, and writhe to and fro more merrily than ever, taking hue from the many tinted windows through which stream the rays from the tripods.[21]

In response, some students focus on the fragility of the festive atmosphere, as interrupted every so often by the sonorous and ominous strikes of the ebony clock. They become fascinated by the metaphorical descriptions of dreams floating in the air, and how these dreams – expressing people's states of mind – would all freeze momentarily as the chimes overtake them. Some students imagine and design masks made of glass elements (see Figure 3.3, left); masks that could break as easily as the dreams, but while breaking would produce a multiple of sharp glass blades, to be used as defensive weapons in the case of the deadly threat. Other students imagine these dreams as stories of people's lives that longed to be shared and heard. In these cases, they design masks that magnify the sense of sound, like huge ears working as extensions of their own ears (see Figure 3.3, right). They not only argue that such masks would give the dreams a voice, but also make sure that the sound of the clock does not get lost during the dream-listening. Fittingly, they craft such masks as movable objects that could additionally work as weapons in case of need.

Observing for words

In a 2021 graduate design studio, students were challenged to incorporate literature into their architecture design process. While the studio's aim focused on the design of an observatory which allows

Figure 3.3 (left) Glass mask designed by student B. Soler; (right) Magnifying sound mask and defensive weapon designed by student J. Conner, Louisiana State University, 2018.

Source: Image of B. Soler and J. Conner with work provided by the authors.

for the curation of two views in a nearby park, literature played an important role in not only jumpstarting the creative process, but also in establishing project tenets. First, students received a list of novellas and short stories. The suggested readings varied tremendously in format, focus, and voice. Students browsed suggestions like Lauren van den Berg's *I Hold a Wolf by the Ears* (2020) and Denis Johnson's *The Largesse of the Sea Maiden* (2018) to George Sunders' *Tenth of December* (2014) and Brandon Taylor's *Filthy Animals* (2021). In a delightful turn of events, some students proposed to engage with poems and prose of their own choosing. Many commented on just how refreshing it was to engage with literature. Students who were fluent in multiple languages found themselves drawn to non-English texts. One student, for example, with a background in woodworking and Italian was able to combine his interests when he selected Carlo Collodi's *The Adventures of Pinocchio* (1883). As providing an opportunity for students to connect with literature in a meaningful way was the key, such unexpected changes were welcome ones. Though these works were sure to take students on wildly different journeys, the short stories had two important aspects in common: they all contained robust descriptions of places and spatial conditions, and they all offered moments of observation. Or put differently, the selected texts not only provided vivid descriptions but also laid the groundwork for the design project to come by helping students understand what it means to observe.

After obtaining a physical copy of their short story, students were asked to doodle or sketch on the page itself while reading the work for the first time. They were encouraged to work freely and quickly, capturing the conditions and leaning on their own interpretation of the words to pull forward ideas about spaces described. This was an intentionally fast and informal task which was motivated by a desire to increase student confidence in drawing and production. As with the undergraduate students, even many graduate students hold on to old habits, find themselves restricted by drawing conventions or overcome by fear of a blank page. By asking students to draw over a pre-printed page eliminated their responsibility to make the first marks. While some pencil work remained in the margins, others began to overtake the page, flooding the printed text on the page with drawings, and linework which speaks to the atmosphere described (see Figure 3.4). Many seized this opportunity as a moment to experiment with different types of drawing media. Working to achieve a wide range of marks and tones, dry media employed ranged from charcoal, chalks, and pastels to pencil and ink. As the week progressed, they were encouraged to read and re-read the work at least two more times in hopes of increasing connections between the words on the page, the unique ideas triggered and the way in which those ideas manifest as drawings. The literary pieces and their content were never seen as a mere background.

With the students now more comfortable drawing over text, they were introduced to *A Humument: A Treated Victorian Novel*, the work of artist Tom Phillips. In 1966, Phillips discovered a relatively unknown 1892 Victorian novel, *A Human Document* by William Hurrell Mallock and set out to transform and revise each page using painting, collage, and "cut-up" techniques inspired by William

TALKING TO LITTLE BIRDIES

Not a peep out of you now
After all the racket early this morning.
Are you begging pardon of me
Hidden up there among the leaves,
Or are your brains momentarily overtaxed?

You savvy a few things I don't:
The overlooked sunflower seed worth a holler;
The traffic of cats in the yard;
Strangers leaving the widow's house,
Tieless and wearing crooked grins.

Or have you got wind of the world's news?
Some new horror I haven't heard about yet?
Which one of you is so bold as to warn me
Our sweet setup is in danger?

Kids are playing soldiers down the road,
Pointing their rifles and playing dead.
Little birdies, are you sneaking wary looks
In the thick foliage
As you watch me go to speak to them?

Figure 3.4 Sketches by student G.W. Klumpp, Louisiana State University, 2021.

Source: Image of G.W. Klumpp's work provided by authors.

Burrough as well as the work of John Cage.[22] Phillips first set out to complete Page 33 of the novel, removing unwanted words and elevating others (see Figure 3.5). The first edition was published in 1970. Ultimately, Phillips produced six editions of this work over the next 50 years, with the final edition in 2017. In a review of the final work, critic Clare Pettit refers to Phillips' approach as "contemplative and

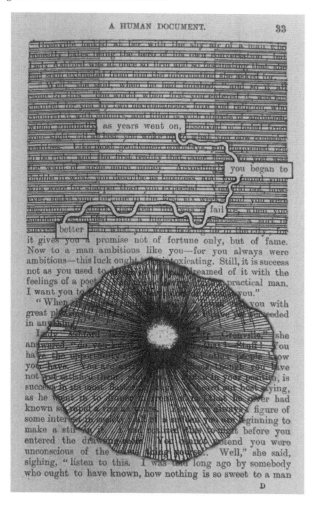

A HUMAN DOCUMENT.   33

as years went on,

you began to

fail

better

it gives you a promise not of fortune only, but of fame.
Now to a man ambitious like you—for you always were
ambitious—this luck ought xicating. Still, it is success
not as you used to eamed of it with the
feelings of a poe practical man.
I want you to ou."
  "When you with
great p eded
in an
   I she
an ou
ha ow
yo ve
not , is
succe ying,
as he had
known figure of
some inte ginning to
make a sti before you
entered the d end you were
unconscious of the Well," she said,
sighing, "listen to this. I long ago by somebody
who ought to have known, how nothing is so sweet to a man

                                                    D

Figure 3.5 Page 33 (Second version 2007) from artist Tom Phillips' *A Humument.*
Source: © 2021 Artists Rights Society (ARS), New York/DACS, London.

solitary" returning to the 367 pages time and time again "'treating'
the book, reworking its pages, overpainting the words."[23]
  With this project in mind, students set out to select a page of text
from the short story they read – a specific page which spoke to them.
Once the students selected the page, the book page is either enlarged
and copied or inverted and Xylene transferred onto a piece of Bristol

or watercolour paper, a surface which will allow them more flexibility with the execution of their drawings. Then, they read and re-read the original text in search of subtexts hidden within the words on the page. Ultimately, they are tasked with making those words visible in the spirit of Tom Phillips by experimenting with drawing, layering, painting, and collaging to remove, downplay, highlight, or emphasise words, phrases, or new short narratives.

The activity may result in an illustrated poem or visual series of dis- and re-articulated phrases which may have a variety of applications beyond the revisited page, itself. If used as a programming assignment, students would be able to lean on the artefact for insights into organising the architectural experience and spaces. Conclusions about the user of the observatory or the surrounding area may be extrapolated from the work if set up as a conceptual phase study. The assignment may even be used to enable students to envision the conditions of one particular space within their design, the creation of a particular atmosphere, experience, or environment.

Concluding remarks

We have found that such literary imagination assignments have consistently proven valuable in helping students proceed with drawings and designs that are grounded in a given context, yet personal and unique. They have been valuable to us, as educators, as the resulting works are surprising and celebrate a wide range of methods, techniques, and interpretations. In his work *The Thinking Hand* (2009), Juhani Pallasmaa discusses the origin of the word "drawing" as coming from the verb "draw out," meaning to bring to light, bring out, the images we have in our head.[24] By engaging literature and literary imagination in architectural education, students are guided to *draw out* and bring to light unique and unexpected conditions of space and architecture. Positioning such assignments in a student's architectural education, the struggle to deal with new techniques and tools becomes embedded in their experience. We believe that if a student's willingness to be "unsettled" dovetails with their understanding of the creative process in a pivotal way, it might have the potential to impact the rest of their architectural path, academic, or professional. We wonder if it can actually instil an instinctive willingness towards tool and process understanding, but also an openness to subvert them or use them unconventionally. Indeed, these drawing exercises led to a burst of imagination for the projects which followed. Many students tackled uncommon architectural programmes which they had never experienced, either as users or designers. Yet, they confronted the challenge uninhibitedly.

Our pedagogical approach, as inspired by research into the intersection of architecture and literature, does not imply that the reading of novels or short stories is the only way to challenge, foster, and think about unconventional approaches to drawing and modelling in architectural education. In the last example, we discuss references from art that could also become part of our literary explorations. Our approach strives primarily to help students engage critically with visual information that is so readily available, protect their developing minds from becoming intimidated, challenge their preconceptions, instil a confidence in their ability to imagine, and introduce them to the richness of interdisciplinary connections. It works to make them understand that their own spatial perceptions – specific and even completely subjective at a first glance – bear a paramount meaning for them as architects; a meaning that should be communicated and shared. In this way, constructing a drawing or building a design, while one's imagination is fuelled by words, necessitates a constant interpretation of these words, a critical "thinking" and "making" process at each step along the way, as each mark on the page (each metaphor or spatial description) can be in essence a project unto itself.

Notes

1 Ricoeur talked about literary imagination in his 1979 article "The Function of Fiction in Shaping Reality," and connected it both to literature and language in general. For more see: Ricoeur, Paul. "The Function of Fiction in Shaping Reality," *Man and World* 12, no. 2 (1979): 123–141.
2 Elaine Scarry, *Dreaming by the Book* (Princeton, NJ: Princeton University Press, 2001), 76.
3 Ibid.
4 Richard Kearney, "Paul Ricoeur and the Hermeneutic Imagination," in *The Narrative Path, The Later Works of Paul Ricoeur*, ed. T. Peter Kemp and David Rasmussen (Cambridge, MA: MIT Press, 1989), 1.
5 Ibid.
6 Paul Ricoeur, "The Function of Fiction in Shaping Reality," *Man and World* 12, no. 2 (1979): 127.
7 Paul Ricoeur, *The Rule of Metaphor, Multi-disciplinary Studies of the Creation of Meaning in Language*, trans. Robert Czerny (Toronto, ON: University of Toronto Press, 1981), 11.
8 Ibid., 12.
9 Harry Francis Mallgrave, *The Architect's Brain: Neuroscience, Creativity and Architecture* (West Sussex: Wiley-Blackwell, 2011), 174.
10 Alberto Pérez-Gómez, *Attunement: Architectural Meaning After the Crisis of Modern Science* (Cambridge: MIT Press, 2016), 197.

11 Anca Matyiku, "Architecture Drawn Out of Bruno Schulz's Poetic Prose," in *Reading Architecture: Literary Imagination and Architectural Experience*, ed. Angeliki Sioli and Yoonchun Jung (New York; London: Routledge, 2018), 114.

12 See: Lisa Landrum. "Varieties of Architectural Imagination," in *Warehouse 25*, ed. Alena Rieger and Ally Pereira-Edwards (Winnipeg, MB: University of Manitoba,, 2016); Klaske Havik, *Urban Literacy, Reading and Writing Architecture* (Rotterdam: nai010 publishers, 2014).

13 Klaske Havik, Urban Literacy, 23.

14 For a set of rules for both instructors and students on how such assignments could be run please see: Angeliki Sioli and Kristen Kelsch, "The Literary Imagination: Drawing Out the Unexpected," in *Theories and Tactics in Architecture and Design*, ed. Samantha Krukowski (London: Intellect Books, 2022), 150-153.

15 The choice of Murakami's novel was inspired by an assignment with similar focus, developed by Thomas Balaban, Michael Jemtrud, Maria Elisa Navarro Morales, Suresh Perera and Pierina Saia, for a first-year design studio (ARCH201) at McGill University's School of Architecture in the fall of 2009.

16 Angeliki Sioli and Kristen Kelsch, ARCH1002 Syllabus, Louisiana State University, Spring 2017 and Spring 2018.

17 Haruki Murakami, *The Wind-Up Bird Chronicle*, trans. Jay Rubin (New York, NY: Vintage Books/Knopf Doubleday) 391.

18 Ibid., 66.

19 Franz Kafka, "The Burrow," in *Franz Kafka Complete Stories* (Berlin: Schocken Books), 332.

20 The full trajectory of this design studio, developed by Angeliki Sioli and built exclusively on interconnections between architecture and literature, was presented at the 108th ASCA Annual Meeting: Open (digital conference) in June 2020 and will appear in the forthcoming proceedings under the title "The Detective-Stories Studio: The Function of Fiction in Shaping Architectural Education".

21 Edgar Allan Poe, "The Masque of the Red Death," in *The Collected Tales and Poems of Edgar Allan Poe* (New York, NY: The Modern Library), 227.

22 It should be noted that Tristan Tzara and Brion Gysin were making cut-ups well before the technique was popularised by William Burroughs, that said, cut-ups are randomly dis-articulated and re-assembled fragments of texts.

23 Clare Pettit, "Strange Labour," in *Times Literary Supplement* (London: Times Literary Supplement, 2017), 10.

24 Juhani Pallasmaa, *The Thinking Hand: Existential and Embodied Wisdom in Architecture* (London: Wiley, 2009), 54.

Bibliography

Havik, Klaske. *Urban Literacy: Reading and Writing Architecture*. Rotterdam: nai010publishers, 2014.

Kearney, Richard. "Paul Ricoeur and the Hermeneutic Imagination." In *The Narrative Path, The Later Works of Paul Ricoeur*, edited by T. Peter Kemp and David Rasmussen, Cambridge, MA: MIT Press, 1989.

Landrum, Lisa. "Varieties of Architectural Imagination." In *Warehouse 25*, edited by Alena Rieger and Ally Pereira-Edwards, Winnipeg, MB: University of Manitoba, 2016.

Mallgrave, Harry Francis. *The Architect's Brain: Neuroscience, Creativity and Architecture*. West Sussex: Wiley-Blackwell, 2011.

Matyiku, Anca. "Architecture Drawn Out of Bruno Schulz's Poetic Prose." In *Reading Architecture: Literary Imagination and Architectural Experience*, edited by Angeliki Sioli and Yoonchun Jung. New York; London: Routledge, 2018.

Murakami, Haruki. *The Wind-Up bird Chronicle*. New York, NY: Vintage Books/Knopf Doubleday, 1998.

Pallasmaa, Juhani. *The Thinking Hand: Existential and Embodied Wisdom in Architecture*. London: Wiley, 2009.

Pettit, Clare. "Strange Labour" In *Times Literary Supplement*. London: Times Literary Supplement, 2017.

Pérez-Gómez, Alberto. *Attunement: Architectural Meaning after the Crisis of Modern Science*. Cambridge, MA: MIT Press, 2016.

Phillips, Tom. *A Humument: A Treated Victorian Novel*. New York, NY: Thames and Hudson, 1997

Poe, Edgar Allan. "The Masque of the Red Death." In *The Collected Tales and Poems of Edgar Allan Poe*. 211–234. New York, NY: The Modern Library, 1992.

Ricoeur, Paul. "The Function of Fiction in Shaping Reality," *Man and World* 12, no. 2 (1979): 123–141.

———. *The Rule of Metaphor, Multi-disciplinary Studies of the Creation of Meaning in Language*. Translated by Robert Czerny. Toronto, ON: University of Toronto Press, 1981.

Scarry, Elaine. *Dreaming by the Book*. Princeton, NJ: Princeton University Press, 2001.

4   Mapping the creative edge

Dialogic pedagogies in architectural education

Kasia Nawratek

Introduction

One of the biggest challenges in architectural education is to antic-
ipate and prepare students for conditions of future practice. As a
vocational discipline, architecture has traditionally strong links with
the profession, and as a result architectural education is a delicate
balancing act responding to the expectations coming from the profession with its current needs and requirements, and anticipating how
they might change, what trends are going to prove the most influential
and lasting, and prepare students for that speculative future.

In creative industries, the edges of disciplines are increasingly
blurred, the ability to negotiate a shared creative vision in collaborative projects becomes a template for future practice, and architecture
is no exception. Therefore, teaching across disciplines and embed-
ding collaboration is a way to position future architects as versatile
and flexible creatives, capable of working in various professional
scenarios.

The Free City Guide student project discussed in this chapter was an
attempt to address this need for collaboration and interdisciplinarity.

The aim of the project was to establish an interdisciplinary
approach to mapping, where conventional mapping techniques used
in architecture meet storytelling, poetry, and film-making, creating a
new layer of expression and understanding of the city. The project was
also an attempt to create a link between my pedagogical practice and
creative writing. As an architect and academic living in the United
Kingdom, I am immersed in English, but my creative writing practice
is in my mother tongue, Polish. This results in a sense of a dual identity, stretched between academia and literature, divided along the use
of two languages. Following this rift, I aimed to highlight the potential of linguistic diversity in the context of university education and

DOI: 10.4324/9781003258933-5

explore the translation as a process of mediation not only between languages but also between visual and verbal forms of expression.

Co.LAB platform

Collaborative Laboratory (Co.LAB) is a live project module at the Birmingham School of Architecture and Design. Since 2011, the module has been a vehicle for transdisciplinary and experimental approach testing disciplinary boundaries and seeking to disrupt conventional design methods. Projects delivered in the module are collaborations with external partners, such as community groups, local authorities, commercial bodies, public institutions, and cultural organisations, as well as freelance creatives.

Each year undergraduate and postgraduate students from architecture and other design courses choose a Co.LAB project led by an academic tutor and an external partner. For 13 weeks students work in small groups and produce an online document, a blog[1] documenting progress and a short film exploring one chosen element or aspect of the project.

The Free City Guide was one of Co.LAB projects in 2017, a collaboration between the architecture school and the School of English involving architecture students (second year undergraduate and first year Master of Architecture) working in small groups with second year undergraduate students from the School of English.

It wasn't a typical Co.LAB project because the collaborative partner was not external, but came from the same faculty. It was, however, an unusual and challenging partnership as architecture typically seeks to collaborate with creative disciplines that share similar modes of expression, usually visual, making the communication between disciplines easier.

Points of departure

There were two main points of departure shaping this project, one considered the spatial condition of Birmingham canals identified as a type of liminal urban space, and the second explored the tension between linguistic representation and spatial thinking. The spaces that inspired the project elude a precise definition and are known under various names. Richard Mabey's book, "The unofficial countryside"[2] explored them from a naturalist's perspective, whereas Gilles Clément put them in a wide category of the Third Landscape,[3] containing not only as different spaces as abandoned urban or rural sites (délaissé), neglected land (friches), shores, swamps, road-sides, and railways embankments, but also national parks and nat-ural reserves. Unattended and free from human interference, with time they become nature's strongholds. Another definition by Alan Berger describes them as drosscape,[4] defined as wastelands left by rapid urbanisation and deindustrialisation. Marion Shoard[5] intro-duced the term Edgelands, describing a ubiquitous but often over-looked type of landscape defined as neither urban nor rural. Finally, it was the book "Edgelands"[6] by poets Michael Symmons Roberts and Paul Farley that gave the project its spatial focus. The book is an attempt to classify various spaces of this often-misunderstood and overlooked type of British landscape in a form of a journey through wastelands, allotments, canals, landfills, woodlands, motorways, and other city edges.

Edgelands' spatial condition can be described as being somewhere in-between, on the edge, on the fringes of something more defined. Their description is often relative, dependent on a more recognisable type of space, and therefore ambiguous. They are often nameless and pushed to the edges of consciousness, our inability to pin them down with a name on a map renders them invisible. They are the blind spots in the collective vision of city dwellers, where the unknown is hiding in plain sight. Unexplored, and potentially dangerous, they remain elusive and uncharted.

My first impression of the post-industrial spaces in Birmingham was their unexpected familiarity, creating another layer of liminal-ity that was not only spatial but also temporal. While exploring these spaces, time and space became somewhat misleading, stretching beyond the familiar now, back to my childhood in a different time and place. I explored this temporal shift of Edgelands in my chil-dren's book,[7] where it can be detected through the freedom to roam the city as experienced by the main character, a seven-year-old boy, who explores the edges of his neighbourhood only with his dog for company. Despite the story being set contemporarily, this points to a different time, when the heavy industry in the area was collapsing, leaving big chunks of the city closed-off but not inaccessible for curi-ous and unsupervised children. This liminality of Edgelands allows for other dimensions to manifest themselves, and in the book it's the main character's vivid imagination that brings them to life. The neigh-bourhood in the story is built around a coalmine, a mixture of XIX century red brick workers' houses, and modern residential high rises overlooking wild meadows and woodlands, hiding ruins of old houses torn down to make space for the never built express way. For the boy, it's the underground that holds the biggest secrets, where deep down, hiding in the mining shafts, ancient monsters lead their secretive lives, monitored by tech-savvy rabbits.

Every attempt to define Edgelands creates a tension between their spatial reality and the linguistic imprecision stemming from the difficulty to categorise and name them. Each new attempt risks further distortion of our understanding of their spatial condition. They seem to possess an uncanny ability to actively avoid description leaving themselves open to interpretation and therefore presenting a unique opportunity to be whatever one wants, or needs them, to be.

Subversive and creative potential of Edgelands

Every time language, or our ability to name something is challenged, a gap appears where new meanings can emerge. If we follow Wittgenstein and accept that limits of our language mean the limits of our world, then this vagueness of Edgelands caused by the incompatibility of language and space is an opportunity for a new perspective – one in which Edgelands are seen as an opportunity to defy the all-encompassing narrative of late capitalism (neoliberalism) relentlessly colonising every aspect of the world and human existence with very precisely defined commodification. From this perspective, drosscape, Edgelands, the Third Landscape, and liminal spaces are not seen as a potential commodity, but as the last spatial line of defence against the dominant capitalist narrative.

Following Rosa Luxemburg, capitalism can only sustain itself through the "(...) continuous and progressive disintegration of non-capitalist organisations."[8] In other words, capitalism is parasitic to external forms of social organisation. It can only sustain itself, if there is something external to it, the outside, that it can latch onto and exploit. As a narrative, it is not only reductive and limiting, but also ubiquitous and permeating every sphere of life and human activity with an all-encompassing, hegemonic narrative of constant growth and commodification.

Boris Groys highlights the role of money in capitalism as a tool for mediation, and contrasts it with language:

> Under capitalist economic conditions, paradox can be interpreted as a conflict of interests, and thus it can be resolved, at least provisionally, by a compromise in the medium of money. In the medium of language, however, paradox can neither be paid off nor consequently disempowered.[9]

In the capitalist narrative, the infinite complexity of the world becomes flattened through the use of money (numbers) in the process of commodification. Whereas language is the source of richness, that acknowledges and highlights paradox (conflict) and allows it to manifest itself.

When the question of how to tame capitalist narrative's expansive nature arises, it's the power of language, that can offer an alternative. Perhaps capitalism can be subverted through the multiplication of subjective, multi-layered and multifaceted narratives celebrating individual, non-replicable experiences. Multiple narrators and meanings have the power to blur and invalidate the idea of one, dominant narrative, opening the world to multiple interpretations and multi-voiced conversations.

This approach is rooted in Mikhail Bakhtin's idea of polyphony,[10] which originated from his reading of the works of Fyodor Dostoevsky. Polyphony, a term borrowed from music, was used by Bakhtin to read Dostoevsky's works as containing multiple voices and perspectives, with their own importance within the novel and able to speak for themselves, sometimes even against the author. Unlike in music, polyphony in literature doesn't strive for harmony. On the contrary, it invites friction and conflict, where opposing points of view are equally important, resulting in a nuanced and fuller picture of the world with all its contradictions and complexities. It invites negotiation and dialogue to all interactions, bringing into focus the entanglement and interdependence of all beings. When applied to architecture, this perspective opens intriguing opportunities as its premise is radically different to a traditional design process where a lone architect, and his – as it would almost always be a man – singular vision is bestowed on the world leaving a mark on its fabric for posterity and "colonising" it with one man's idea.

Following Bakhtin again, this could be described as a monologic model and is increasingly being challenged by more collaborative, non-hierarchical, and inclusive forms of practice.[11] This is caused not only by the increasing complexity of projects, where the input by various specialists put the architect into a more dialogical position, but also by the need for a more inclusive design process, where hierarchies are flattened and agency expanded to include more stakeholders in the production of space.

When considered from a polyphonic perspective, due to their elusiveness, Edgelands appear as spaces charged with creative potential, where nothing is fixed and even time becomes warped, offering a glimpse into a future where crumbling infrastructure is taken over by nature, a world where the catastrophe has already happened, but life carries on regardless, with humans or without. It is a post-apocalyptic and post-capitalist vision of Edgelands becoming portals to unknown, alternative timelines.

Even if not labelled as such, Edgelands have long served as an inspiration for artists and writers. One notable example would be the Zone appearing in the film Stalker (1979)[12] based on the novel "Roadside Picnic"[13] by Soviet-Russian authors Arkady and Boris Strugatsky and directed by Andrei Tarkovsky. The real-life Edgelands of an abandoned hydropower power plant, a chemical factory and a highway bridge in Estonia, became the Zone in the film, a mysterious place supposedly visited by aliens and possessing wish-granting properties. These industrial spaces were not designed for human habitation, their architecture merely tolerating human beings as maintenance providers and reluctantly leaning in to accommodate their scale and needs. Its inhuman scale not only creates an atmosphere of alienation but also thrill, as the unfamiliar scale and forms are open to speculations what the architecture created by Others might look like, and who might they be. The environmental destruction is another theme associated with Edgelands as they can be often found in the vicinity, or at the sites of industrial production. The vision of the future in the Blade Runner films, particularly the spaces in Blade Runner 2049,[14] depicts a dystopian world shaped by the environmental collapse.

A less desolate, but nonetheless cautionary vision can be found in the Japanese anime film "Pom Poko"[15] telling a story of tanuki[16] desperately trying to survive as the expanding cities destroy their natural habitat. In the Japanese folklore, tanuki are the mischievous shape-shifters, able to turn into humans at will, occupying the threshold between nature and the city, and between reality and the magical realm. When the expansive urbanisation upsets the delicate balance of their environment, they struggle to adapt. This conflict between urbanisation and nature is a spatial representation of the deeper struggle – tanuki symbolise the connection to the idealised and mythical past, where nature and people coexisted peacefully and crossing the boundaries from the magical realm to our reality was still possible. When the growing city devours their home, tanuki are forced to turn into humans permanently and it comes at a price of their magical abilities. The choice between nature-magic-past and the city-civilisation-future creates a profound sense of loss which is the main theme explored in the film. The in-between creatures occupying the spaces on the verge of civilisation embody the potential of edge conditions, how blurry, undefined boundaries allow for shifts in meaning and negotiations of narratives.

In Sean Baker's 2017 film "The Florida Project," sunlit Floridian Edgelands are seen through the eyes of a six-year-old Moonee. The pastel colours of the motel she lives in with her struggling mother, the neon signs of the drive-throughs and petrol stations, the half-wild green spaces she explores with her friends hold more wonder than the nearby Disneyland, the epicentre of her world gracing it with a magical, yet unreachable, glow. These are the spaces where children's imagination creates an alternative Disneyland, full of promise and invisible to adults.

The subversive potential of Edgelands is explored in the photography series "Girl pictures" by Justine Kurland.[17] In her photographs, groups of teenage girls, possibly runaways, roam freely the edges of American suburbs, breaking free from expectations of where and what young women ought to be. They appear on the backdrop of infrastructure or overgrown wilderness, that somehow suggests a proximity of the city. In this narrative, girls are supportive of each other, forming free roaming groups. They seem to tap into something primal and revolutionary, as they appear to be fully in sync with each other and their own bodies. They emerge free and unstoppable from the fringes of cities, empowered by their connection to nature and taking the opportunity of overlooked Edgelands to form alliances. They seem to have a plan and it might involve taking over the world. In this vision, Edgelands emerge as subversive spaces of female empowerment, youth rebellion, and revolutionary political potential.

Dialogism and polyphony in architectural education

Architectural education is actively trying to respond to the need for a more collaborative approach, but it finds itself in a difficult position as its roots are in the monologic tradition where individuality, originality, and leadership skills are championed and expected from successful candidates and alumni. Students arrive at the university with a mindset oriented towards individual achievements, and this trajectory continues as the majority of assessments are individual. In the course of their education, architecture students are rarely given opportunities to form creative partnerships or collectives when working towards major assessment points.

On the other hand, students themselves are often reluctant to engage in group projects, on the surface embracing the collaborative spirit, but struggling with the ingrained need to be recognised and assessed for their individual efforts. In their view collaboration is a particularly limiting constraint to their creativity and self-realisation. From a pedagogical point of view, this is not necessarily something to be discouraged, but it poses an interesting question of how to balance the drive for creative self-expression with a more dialogic approach.

Perhaps this question should be reframed and viewed not as a binary choice between self-expression and collaboration. Instead of falling into the trap of binary thinking, perhaps we should ask: What is the role of the architect in the complex web of often opposing interests of all actors involved in the design process?, and more importantly in the context of education in creative subjects: How to navigate it? A polyphonic perspective, where all voices are valued and given space gives clues how this could be approached. In the context of the design studio, it might also mean embracing the actual voices of the students through the languages they speak to allow their cultural heritage to be heard.

The built-in feature of the polyphonic approach is the act of negotiation, which may help embracing the unpredictable nature of the design process. This uncertainty is often a source of anxiety for students, who lack confidence needed to navigate it. Even when tasked with recording their design process, students tend to gloss over failed experiments, presenting a false narrative of a linear decision sequence neatly leading to the final product. It is, however, a stifling mindset, one that sanitises the design process of its inherent messiness, and devalues experimentation, resulting in a rush to present final conclusions, without sufficient testing and exploration of creative avenues available on the way. This is also not reflective of the contemporary practice, where the networked working requires constant negotiation and embracing different points of view. When applied to the design process in architectural education, the polyphonic approach is helpful in framing group work as a dynamic process between active participants, where the findings of the explorations are unpredictable and opened for creative possibilities at every stage.

Free City Guide was an opportunity for students to experience a different mode of working, where individual voices needed to join a conversation and abandon rigid ideas of authorship and creative control. As a starting point, this is challenging and requires a fundamental change in understanding of the group work. In this mode, individual contributions are impossible to distinguish, and the final outcome offers a new, unexpected quality, going beyond the initial expectations and predictions. This is, however, a perilous process that can only lead to successful outcomes under two conditions: firstly, students must be given enough time to experiment, and secondly, they need to feel confident enough, to allow their experiments to fail before they find their way through the process. Time is needed for students to work out the interpersonal dynamics of their teams and to give them the opportunity to roam freely knowing, that any unsuccessful experiment, is an opportunity to learn without consequences.

Students' confidence can be propped by the lack of pressure to perform and meet set expectations, which can be especially liberating for students from professionally accredited courses like architecture, where a predetermined set of standards can impose a rigid framework of outcomes that must be achieved at every stage. One of Co.LAB's main strengths was a creative environment offered to students, where they were in charge of the direction of their explorations disregarding disciplinary boundaries and set expectations. In the process, the work emerged free from disciplinary labels, but it was only possible because all disordered and unsuccessful moments were embraced as expected, and even welcomed, elements of the process. In the most successful projects, the authorship was shared and blurred, and individual contributions are almost impossible to distinguish.

"Truth is not born nor is it found inside the head of an individual person, it is born between people collectively searching for truth, in the process of their dialogic interaction,"[18] when applied to design process, Bakhtin's description of the importance of relationships between people, becomes a template for collaborative modes of working in creative disciplines, where "truth" becomes a vision of the world forged in this process. The focus shifts from individuals to the relationships between them and to the act of exchange, active listening, and negotiation. Bakhtin's dialogic approach is then radically contextual, all beings (voices) are seen not to be existing in themselves, but are defined through their relations.

Another important factor in the project was a multidisciplinary set of tutors (an architect/writer, a poet, a geographer/writer, and a filmmaker) offering a variety of approaches, modes of thinking, and communication. The need for constant negotiation between different modes of thinking within student groups, and between tutors and students, created a working environment defined by dialogic approach, a dynamic and changeable situation, where it was easier for students to reject the linearity of the creative process and embrace its messiness, openness, and uncertainty.

Free City Guide project brief

Students were tasked with preparing an unreliable guide to the Free City of Birmingham. The unreliability of the guide was a reference to the character of Marco Polo from Italo Calvino's "Invisible cities"[19] who describes various fictional cities from his journeys, but which also tell something true about Marco Polo's home city of Venice. The project brief for students advised:

> Your role taken up for the project will be different to the urban explorer and to the figure of the flaneur (and his recently introduced female counterpart, the flaneuse), as you will explore the city through narratives. (…), you will assume the role of a storyteller creating the city through your and other people's stories, similarly to Italo Calvino's Marco Polo in "Invisible cities", where he maps the city of Venice as the most unreliable of narrators, a skilful creator of myths and yet never guilty of lying.[20]

Walking was used as a mapping tool, and the aim was to create multi-layered and multifaceted narratives exploring individual experiences through urban exploration.

Interdisciplinary approach and its challenges

The theoretical framework was established by the author, a writer and an architect, but the project was co-led by a team of tutors and collaborators from other disciplines. Derek Littlewood, a poet from the School of English provided a language focussed perspective, Tom Keeley, is a self-described topographic practitioner, "working between architectures, geographies, landscapes and histories through practice-based research, design projects and site-specific writing"[21] opened the investigations to place-writing practices. Poet Liz Berry was invited for a poetry reading and her canal murder ballad "The Black Delph Bride,"[22] written in the Black Country dialect highlighted the diversity of accents in the United Kingdom, opening a discussion about local identity, linguistic variety of English accents, and introduced the idea of place writing. Robert Lawson from the School of English led a workshop on poetry in the Scots language, and Pip Piper, a filmmaker, led film-making and editing workshops.

The interdisciplinary setting aimed to open the field of exploration and following Marilyn Stember, its ambition was to achieve an integrated approach, and even a modification of the disciplinary boundaries: (interdisciplinarity) "(...) requires more or less integration and even modification of the disciplinary contributions while the inquiry or teaching is proceeding."[23]

As Albena Yaneva and Bruno Latour put it: "Everybody knows—and especially architects, of course—that a building is not a static object but a moving project, and that even once it is has been built, it ages, it is transformed by its users, modified by all of what happens inside and outside, and that it will pass or be renovated, adulterated and transformed beyond recognition."[24] It situates architecture in a unique position as a discipline requiring constant "translation" and mediation between the physical realm, in which all buildings exist, and ever-changing set of regulations, cultural conventions, and socio-economic contexts that somehow conditions architects to disregard disciplinary boundaries and conventions.

It is not unusual then for a project in an architecture school to use an interdisciplinary approach. As architecture tends to foray into other disciplines regularly, it takes advantage of its wide-ranging field of interest, reaching as far as philosophy, social sciences, building science, but also anthropology and art. This often results in a "parasitic" approach of architects borrowing from other disciplines, but in the Free City Guide it was replaced by a more collaborative and balanced working relationship where different disciplinary toolkits were shared and appropriated to new uses.

The process of exploration and constructing a response to the brief was not without challenges. The first few weeks were difficult for students, who not only had to engage with unfamiliar themes and modes of working, but also establish a good working relationship with their groupmates and a group of tutors. However, as soon as they embraced the openness of the brief and creative opportunities it offered, they took full ownership of their creative process. Architecture students in particular found the open brief liberating, as the course tends to leave very little space for experimentation beyond architecture.

Language vs space

In literature, language is the subject and the medium of creative explorations, whereas architecture engages with space. The challenge of accurately communicating spatial conditions is embedded in all architectural projects. It is the reason why architectural modes of representation are primarily visual to avoid the danger of misinterpretation.

In architecture, it is crucial to communicate spatial conditions effectively and accurately. The basic set of orthographic drawings:

plans, sections, and elevations, is an established, though increasingly challenged by new digital technologies, mode of communication of architects. Therefore, the innovation and the challenge in the Free City Guide project were the exploration of the relationship between space and language, which harnessed the creative potential of the tension created by the distorting power of language and its inability to fully and definitively describe the world.

Architect Bernard Tschumi[25] went even further, describing this tension as "(...) the mutually exclusive systems of words and stone, between the literary program and the architectural text." In Joyce's Garden (1976), a student project he led in London, participants used Finnegan's Wake as the programme for an architectural proposal in Covent Garden. This project embraced the incompatibility of language and space, and the tension between them was harnessed to generate architectural responses. It also aimed to critique the functionalist approach and free architecture from the constraints of programme. This embracing of conflict between narratives, and as Tschumi names them "texts," is a similar approach to the polyphonic method and demonstrates its potential as a design method.

Student projects

Free City Beast

This project started with a poem written by students, where the titular beast represents the industrial legacy of Birmingham, hiding in the canals' infrastructure and embodying the city's identity and history.

In this project students asked, if the beast could evolve or if it's destined to remain linguistically inert forever. To answer this question, the poem was translated into Romanian, Persian, and Russian by respective native speakers and then translated back to English.

In the first translation, a series of diagrams identified words without direct equivalents, those with ambiguous or indirect translation. Each diagram then placed a word from the original poem in English that proved to be difficult to translate, and surrounded it with a ring of synonyms and closely related words. Then each translator chose a word from the ring closest in meaning in their respective languages and highlighted it in the final English version. This close reading of the translation process visualised how the original poem changed and morphed through the first translation process and how the second translation back to English highlighted divergent words and subsequent shifts in meaning.

The film[26] accompanying the project demonstrated this process. Each translator read the poem in their language and highlighted the fluctuation in meaning. With each iteration, small shifts in meaning occurred, demonstrating how using different languages subtly changes the perception of the world.

The project reflected the experience of non-native English speakers in the English-speaking environment and revealed how the language impacts users' understanding of the world. It also revealed how the language we use to describe the world becomes a lens filtering what we see. The distortion becomes apparent when revealed through a process of translation, as discrepancies and inaccuracies occurring in the translation process reveal reality that is not monolithic and fixed, but constantly changing and alive with multiple meanings. The Free City Beast project positioned the translation process as cultural exchange, highlighting the ever evolving and alive nature of language.

From the point of view of architecture, this haptic connection between language and space added another dimension to understanding of space by architecture students. For English students, the experience of grounding in physical space and using visualisation to gain an insight into the translation process was an unexpected outcome of this project.

This project resonated with the whole group of students involved in the Free City project. The focus on difference, in this case the linguistic richness among the group, highlighted the linguistic and cultural diversity of the group. The Birmingham City University student cohort is one of the more diverse in the country[27]: in 2019, 46% were from non-white British and international background. For architecture students in particular, this acknowledgement and celebration of their native languages proved very important and it also included international students who found space to express and share their cultural identity with their peer group. This was further supported by the exploration of local accents in the Black Country through the poetry of Liz Berry, and the Scots language led by Robert Lawson, which opened the discussion on inclusion and linguistic diversity for native English speakers within their native language too.

Portal

Following a similar path to the Free City Beast project, students wrote a poem inspired by their walks along the canal. Initially searching for local urban myths, they reached deeper and referenced Celtic

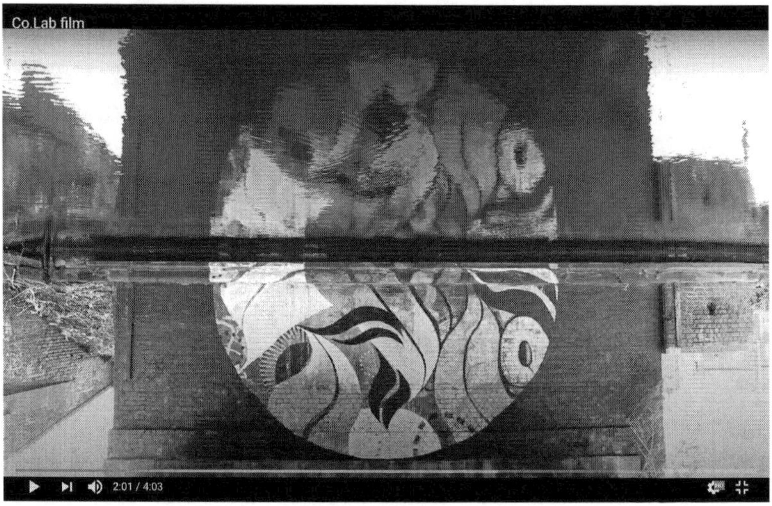

Figure 4.1 A screenshot from "portal," Muhammad Yasin Ali, YouTube.

mythology, where still water was seen as a magical screen separating reality and the realm of gods. This liminal quality of water led them to identifying it as another type of Edgelands.

A film[28] illustrating the poem was a meditation on the liminal quality of Birmingham canals and through editing and image manipulation, it attempted to reveal a different reality apparently lurking in seemingly mundane spaces. Physical space of Birmingham canals was depicted to be this threshold, an edge, where gritty urban reality meets a hidden mythical realm and the fabric of reality is so thin, it reveals a different world behind it.

The film referenced the myth of Narcissus, playing with the images reflected in the water and by separating the reality from its reflection, it explored the idea of reflections as gateways to another world with its own time, disjointed from our reality.

"Portal" was one of the most successful outcomes of the project, an affective short film that conjured an otherworldly atmosphere and captured the promise and menace of the canal site.

The good air

The project took Italo Calvino's short story "The good air" from the collection "Marcovaldo"[29] and deconstructed the text to reveal a different story reflecting an experience of living in Birmingham. Students used storyboarding to retell the original story through a film,[30] and used their experiences of newcomers living in unfamiliar Birmingham to explore how the juxtaposition of the visual narrative and the original text created new meanings and enriched each other. This project highlighted experiences of international students moving to the United Kingdom and exploring the city as outsiders.

The disjunction between the visual narrative and the original Italo Calvino's story reflected the experience of non-native speakers immersed in a new, unfamiliar space, trying to make sense of it in a language that is not their mother tongue. The sense of otherness and dissociation was then exacerbated by the use of different languages and the distortion caused by the multiplication of meanings.

Teaching as creative practice

Tracing the entwined strands of my creative practice and teaching, I had to confront my preconceptions towards my own practice. The fascination with liminal urban landscapes inspired by my childhood in a post-industrial and post-socialist city in South-Western Poland was an inspiration for my children's book and then found its way into my teaching practice through the Free City Guide project. The ideas explored in this project became foundations for a theoretical framework based on a polyphonic approach expanded to include non-human voices. This post-humanist approach opened my investigations to formulate a basis for a design driven climate crisis response underpinned by inclusivity discourses and rooted in feminist methodology of care. As a result, it directed my interests towards environmental humanities and shaped my current pedagogical approach in the design studio.

I first tested this framework at a Master of Architecture course at the University of Sheffield, where I led a design studio exploring the role of post-industrial urban spaces as potential biodiversity hubs.[31] It later became a theoretical basis for a new atelier I co-founded at Manchester School of Architecture (MSA, 2021) focussing on climate crisis response. The Free City Guide project found its direct continuation in a Research Methods module at the MSA (2021/2022). In this module, I lead a series of deep mapping workshops with elements of creative writing for Master of Architecture students. This project is exploring Manchester Edgelands using the polyphonic approach and collaborative modes of working.

Looking back, it is impossible to detangle the two practices – my creative writing and pedagogical practice become one strand, where they inform and shape each other. As in the creative process, where uncertainty is a feature, not an anomaly, in my teaching practice various threads emerged, evolved, became entangled with each other and formed a pattern, or a common thread that can only be traced from the distance. In the close up, however, the picture is unfocussed and does not present a controlled and unified vision. This process generated many lose ends that may, or may not, become a start for new explorations in the future.

When positioned this way, teaching becomes an important part of the creative practice as an active, not merely reflective, element. This also introduces students to the idea of the creative practice as a journey, where personal development is neither separate nor a side effect of creative work as I evidenced in this chapter on my example.

Combining creating practice with teaching is a unique opportunity to establish a true community of practice for tutors and students. However, for it to be successful, it requires a different positioning of tutors and students within the studio dynamics. Creative trajectories of students and tutors are different, but they can converge at points where they can propel and strengthen each other. In those moments, students and tutors work alongside, the hierarchy is flattened and a sense of shared purpose and direction of exploration creates an empowering environment where all contributions are valued. Design studio is then a testing ground of ideas and methods, where a new vision of the world is forged, and teaching and creative practices inform and enrich each other.

It is, therefore, important to make space for various creatives and practicing architects in architectural education to harness this richness and use it to position architecture schools as forward-thinking, constantly testing, and pushing disciplinary boundaries.

Conclusions

A polyphonic approach rooted in the thought of Mikhail Bakhtin, combined with collaborative and interdisciplinary modes of working, forms the basis of a pedagogical and theoretical platform used in my teaching practice. It stems from the need to prepare students for future practice, where disciplinary boundaries are blurred and collaborative projects require a dialogic approach and the ability to negotiate a creative vision with other disciplines involved in the process.

This approach was tested in the Free City Guide project, where architecture and English students collaborated with a multidisciplinary tutor team involving an architect/writer, a poet, an architectural historian/writer, and a filmmaker. The project considered Edgelands, a type of landscape described by poets Michael Symmons Roberts and Paul Farley, and focused on Birmingham canals. Edgelands were positioned as spaces with a creative and subversive potential, where their ability to avert precise categorisation opens the possibility to create multiple narratives defying and subverting the all-encompassing capitalist narrative of commodification. Through multiplication of subjective narratives and languages, the project opened the possibility of multiple perceptions of the world, at the same time validating all languages and accents spoken by students and recognising the linguistic and cultural diversity of the group. For a diverse cohort taking part in the project, it turned out to be an empowering moment.

The brief outlined the field of exploration and grounded the project theoretically, but allowed students to formulate their response without imposing any formal, methodological, or theoretical expectations. Each student group formulated their interpretation of the brief and chose a direction of explorations. The openness of the brief resulted in a variety of outputs and directions of exploration.

The ideas underpinning the project were a starting point for further investigations and became foundations of my pedagogical approach which I further developed to include post-humanist perspective, allowing me to respond not only to diversity among humans, but also to include non-human actors. This approach further evolved into a design driven climate crisis response underpinned by inclusivity discourses and pointing my further theoretical and pedagogical explorations towards environmental humanities.

Using my experience of the creative writing influencing my teaching practice, I argue for the inclusion of creative practitioners in the architectural pedagogy and demonstrate how entwined creative and pedagogical practices can together become a synergic force of innovation. It is also possible to establish a community of practice and synergy between creative trajectories of tutors and students, but it requires flattening of the hierarchies in the design studio and creating conditions for the emergence of dialogic relationships. From this perspective, teaching can be recognised not as merely a reflection of other creative activities, but a creative practice itself.

Notes

1 Collaborative Laboratory, "Category Archives: Free City Guide," *student blog*, accessed October 25, 2021, https://collaborative-laboratory. org/category/free-city-guide/.

2 Richard Mabey, *The Unofficial Countryside* (Wimborne Minster: Dovecote, 2010).

3 Gilles Clément, "The Third Landscape," accessed October 25, 2021, http://www.gillesclement.com/art-454-tit-The-Third-Landscape.

4 Alan Berger, *Drosscape. Wasting Land in Urban America* (New York: Princeton Architectural Press, 2006).

5 Marion Shoard, "Edgelands," *The Land Magazine,* accessed January 24, 2021, https://www.thelandmagazine.org.uk/articles/Edgelands.

6 Paul Farley and Michel Symmons Roberts, *Edgelands* (London: Vintage Books, 2012).

7 Kasia Nawratek, *Kresek, Bartek i całkiem zwyczajny początek* (Warszawa: Agencja Edytorska EZOP, 2016).

8 Rosa Luxemburg, *The Accumulation of Capital,* trans. Agnes Schwarzschild (New Haven: Yale University Press, 1951), 471.

9 Boris Groys, *The Communist Postscript* (London: Verso Books, 2010). Kindle edition, Loc 778.

10 Andrew Robinson, "In Theory Bakhtin: Dialogism, Polyphony and Heteroglossia," *Ceasefire,* July 29, 2011, accessed January 24, 2021, https://ceasefiremagazine.co.uk/in-theory-bakhtin-1/.

11 Nikole Bouchard, "Collective Imagination: In Conversation with Maria Lisogorskaya of Assemble," in *Waste Matters*, ed. Nikole Bouchard (New York: Routledge, 2020), 180–201.

12 *Stalker*, directed by Andrei Tarkovsky (Mosfilm, 1979).

13 Boris Strugatsky and Arkady Strugatsky, *Roadside Picnic: Take of the Troika*, trans. Antonina W. Bouis (London: Macmillan, 1977).

14 *Blade Runner 2049*, directed by Denis Villeneuve (Alcon Entertainment, 2017).

15 *Pom Poko*, directed by Isao Takahata (Studio Ghibli, 1984).

16 Japanese racoon dogs.

17 Justine Kurland, "Justine Kurland Reflects on Her Photographs of Teenage Girl Runaways," *aperture*, July 2020, https://aperture.org/featured/justine-kurland-girl-pictures/.

18 Mikhail Bakhtin, *Problems of Dostoevsky's Poetics*, trans. Caryl Emerson (Minneapolis: University of Minnesota Press, 1984), 110.

19 Italo Calvino, *Invisible Cities,* trans. William Weaver (London: Vintage Random House, 1997).

20 Kasia Nawratek, *Free City Guide* project brief, unpublished, Birmingham School of Architecture and Design, 2017.

21 Tom Keeley, "Topographic Practice," *Keeley Travel*, accessed January 24, 2021, https://www.keeleytravel.com/information.

22 Liz Berry, "The Black Delph Bride," *The Poetry Society*, accessed January 24, 2021, https://poetrysociety.org.uk/poems/the-black-delph-bride/.

23 Stember, Marilyn. "Advancing the social sciences through the interdisciplinary enterprise," *The Social Science Journal* 28, no. 1 (1991): 5.

24 Albena Yaneva and Bruno Latour, "Give Me a Gun and I Will Make All Buildings Move: An ANT's View of Architecture Explorations in Architecture: Teaching, Design, Research," in *Explorations in Architecture: Teaching, Design, Research*, ed. Reto Geiser (Basel: Birkhäuser Verlag Ag, 2008), 80.

25 Joyce's Garden, "Bernard Tschumi Architects/Projects," *Joyce's Garden*, accessed October 2, 2021, http://www.tschumi.com/projects/49/#.
26 "Free City Beast Film," April 3, 2017, accessed October 2, 2021, https://www.youtube.com/watch?v=czaIbs9TbKQ.
27 "Annual Equality, Diversity and Inclusion Report 2018/19," Birmingham City University, accessed October 27, 2021, https://bcuassets.blob.core.windows.net/docs/csu2020049-edi-annual-report-v10-highres-06-07-20-132398932962257811.pdf.
28 "Co.Lab film," April 3, 2017, Muhammad Yasin Ali, accessed October 2, 2021, http://www.youtube.com/watch?v=y2OzNrEqJsk.
29 Italo Calvino, *Marcovaldo,* trans. William Weaver (London: Vintage, 2002).
30 Collaborative Laboratory, "Final video," *student blog*, accessed October 25, 2021, https://collaborative-laboratory.org/2017/04/03/final-video/.
31 Kasia Nawratek, "Hope in the Burning World," in *Design Studio 2021 Volume 1: Everything Needs to Change*, ed. Sofie Pelsmakers and Nick Newman (London: RIBA Publishing, 2021), 86–97.

Bibliography

Baker, Sean, director. 2017. *The Florida Project*. Cre Film, Freestyle Picture Company, Cinereach, June Pictures.
Bakhtin, Mikhail. *Problems of Dostoevsky's Poetics*. Translated by Caryl Emerson. Minneapolis, MN: University of Minnesota Press, 1984.
Berger, Alan. *Drosscape: Wasting Land in Urban America*. New York, NY: Princeton Architectural Press, 2006.
Berry, Liz. *Black Country*. London: Chatto & Windus, 2014.
Bouchard, Nikole. "Collective Imagination: In Conversation with Maria Lisogorskaya of Assemble." In *Waste Matters*, edited by Nikole Bouchard, 180–201. New York, NY: Routledge, 2020.
Calvino, Italo. *Invisible Cities*. Translated by William Weaver. London: Vintage Random House, 1997.
Calvino, Italo. *Marcovaldo*. Translated by William Weaver. London: Vintage Random House, 2002.
Farley, Paul and Michael Symmons Roberts. *Edgelands*. London: Vintage Books, 2012.
Groys, Boris. *The Communist Postscript*. London: Verso Books, 2010.
Kurland, Justine. "Justine Kurland Reflects on Her Photographs of Teenage Girl Runaways." *aperture*, July 2020. https://aperture.org/featured/justine-kurland-girl-pictures/
Luxemburg, Rosa. *The Accumulation of Capital*. Translated by Agnes Schwarzschild. New Haven, CT: Yale University Press, 1951.
Mabey, Richard. *The Unofficial Countryside*. Wimborne Minster: Dovecote, 2010.
Nawratek, Kasia. *Kresek, Bartek i całkiem zwyczajny początek*. Warszawa: Agencja Edytorska EZOP, 2016.

Nawratek, Kasia. "Hope in the Burning World." In *Design Studio 2021 Volume 1: Everything Needs to Change*, edited by Sofie Pelsmakers and Nick Newman, 86–97. London: RIBA Publishing, 2021.

Robinson, Andrew. "In Theory Bakhtin: Dialogism, Polyphony and Heteroglossia." *Ceasefire*, July 29, 2011. Accessed January 24, 2021. https://ceasefiremagazine.co.uk/in-theory-bakhtin-1/

Shoard, Marion. "Edgelands." *The Land Magazine*. Accessed January 24, 2021. https://www.thelandmagazine.org.uk/articles/edgelands

Stember, Marilyn. "Advancing the social sciences through the interdisciplinary enterprise." *The Social Science Journal* 28, no. 1 (1991): 1–14.

Strugatsky, Boris and Arkady Strugatsky. *Roadside Picnic: Take of the Troika*. Translated by Antonina W. Bouis. London: Macmillan, 1977.

Takahata, Isao, director. 1984. *Pom Poko*. Studio Ghibli.

Tarkovsky, Andrei, director. 1979. *Stalker*. Mosfilm.

Villeneuve, Denis, director. 2017. *Blade runner 2049*. Alcon Entertainment.

Yaneva, Albena and Bruno Latour. "Give me a Gun and I will Make All Buildings Move: An ANT's View of Architecture." In *Explorations in Architecture: Teaching, Design, Research*, edited by Reto Geiser, 80–89. Basel: Birkhäuser Verlag Ag, 2008.

5 Spoken matter

Towards a specific vocabulary for architectural design and description

Nicolai Bo Andersen and
Victor Boye Julebæk

Introduction

In his inaugural address as director of IIT in 1938, Ludwig Mies van der Rohe stated, "[t]hus each material has its specific characteristics that one must get to know in order to work with it. This is no less true of steel and concrete."[1] To Mies, it is not so much the material itself, but rather the way it is used that is important. He continues, "[e]ach material is only worth what we make of it,"[2] arguing that we must understand materials in order to become familiar with the "spiritual [intellectual] position in which we stand."[3] However, it seems as if most architecture today is either concerned with spectacular concepts and instant but superfluous effects, or the opposite, that which provides an anaesthetic poverty of experience which "finds its parallel in modern architecture, in glass-and-steel buildings on whose smooth surfaces the inhabitant cannot leave any traces, any memory,"[4] as described by Beatriz Colomina when discussing the relation between the body and design. The architect's material vocabulary seems limited, architecture seems to have lost the connection to the body, and experiential effects are seemingly not often verbalised.[5]

"Material effect" is a complex and ambiguous notion that includes both tangible and intangible values. The performances and material effects of buildings may not only be regarded as the means by which a building accomplishes practical purposes, but likewise, how it gives them "legible articulation."[6] As such, the term "material effect" concerns the technical, mechanical, and chemical properties of a material, as well as the experienced qualities created through embodied interaction. In the work of Agnes Martin, the "[...] paintings exert themselves differently, depending on their line, their pattern, and the quality of the ground colour on the canvas."[7] In a careful phenomenological

DOI: 10.4324/9781003258933-6

reading, Kasha Linville describes how the experience of the canvases changes as the viewing distance changes. According to Linville, "[a]t close range, you can feel her hand moving," while "[...] they go atmospheric very quickly as you move back from the painting" and "[...] as you step back even further, the painting closes down entirely, becoming completely opaque."[8] In the perspective of the architect, Peter Zumthor states, "[m]aking architecture is [...] less about form, and more about the relation between the architectural material body and the body of us – human beings."[9] Asking what we mean when we speak of architectural quality, he points out that, "[t]o a large degree, designing is based on understanding and establishing systems of order. Yet I believe that the essential substance of the architecture we seek proceeds from feeling and insight."[10] It follows that, to the experienced artist and architect, phenomena and material effects are easily experienced, and definitely operational, but somehow difficult to explain.

We experience architecture as we interact with and navigate the world every day – without giving it a second thought. As such, our knowledge of architecture may largely be considered tacit as "we can know more than we can tell."[11] This "tacit knowledge," as described by Michael Polanyi, is difficult to articulate in words. However, where one may not consciously reflect on the tacit effects of architecture in daily life, practitioners articulate architectural knowledge daily, as do teachers and students of architecture.[12]

At the Royal Danish Academy – Architecture: Master's Programme in Cultural Heritage, Transformation and Conservation (KTR), architectural phenomenological description is used as a method to present experienced phenomena and architectural effects in text and drawings.[13] The combination of investigation, description, and making, as presented here, allows for an approach to architectural design in which students reflect through a form of open hermeneutical dialogue between a spoken language and a material language. It seems, however, that in schools of architecture, as well as in architectural practice in general, the material language as well as the verbal communication of material qualities lacks precision.

Experiencing architecture

In his influential lecture "Material Effects," Carl Petersen describes how we experience physical material. Here, he points out that shape, colour, proportion, and material effects are the four most important elements in the forming arts, including sculpture and architecture.

Describing the surface character of different materials, he points out how one may experience, for instance, two competing surfaces in polished granite. According to Petersen, underneath the shiny surface defining the overall geometry is a landscape made up of the material parts, doubling the surface and "weakening" the form. Describing how "[...] the observer grows uncertain and doubtful if the artist vacillates and employs vague or fortuitous effects,"[14] Petersen's emphasis seems to be on experience over form, as the approach appears to be concerned with materials as they manifest themselves in an embodied perspective. The precise vocabulary (e.g. clear, compact, firm, dry, vague, uncertain, bright, smooth, clear, compact, dead, cloying, weak) that Petersen uses to describe the material effects can be interpreted as not only the surface qualities of the material but also a kind of embodied communication with the material.

In his significant book *Experiencing Architecture*, Steen Eiler Rasmussen develops a more systematic description of how we experience architecture. To Rasmussen, throughout our upbringing we achieve a sensitive, bodily understanding of the world that we unconsciously use when experiencing a work of architecture. Rasmussen argues that "[b]y a variety of experiences [the perceiver] quite instinctively learns to judge things according to weight, solidity, texture and heat conductibility."[15] In other words, we experience architecture physically, through embodied participation, even before we are aware of it intellectually. Although his descriptions may be deemed exemplary, Rasmussen discusses how the essence of architecture is difficult to express in even the most precise descriptions: "[j]ust as we do not notice the individual letters in a word but receive a total impression of the idea the word conveys, we generally are not aware of what it is that we perceive but only of the conception created in our minds when we perceive it."[16] To Rasmussen, architecture is a meaningful language in its own right where "[e]xternal features become a means for communicating feelings and moods from one person to another."[17]

Rasmussen's perspective on architecture as embodied communication resonates well with Maurice Merleau-Ponty's observations on the phenomenon of expression and speech. To Merleau-Ponty, a phenomenon is a basic layer of experience, "a whole already pregnant with an irreducible meaning,"[18] in which the body is given in a dynamic field of perception and where the senses intercommunicate by opening onto the structure of a thing. As pointed out by Romdenh-Romluc, to Merleau-Ponty, the expression of thought, including language, music, painting, and physical gestures, is essentially embodied, as "there is no fundamental difference between modes of expression."[19]

In the same way as "the orator does not think before speaking, nor even while speaking, [as] his speech is his thought, [...] the listener does not form concepts on the basis of signs."[20] In Merleau-Ponty's concept of embodied being (*être-au-monde*), the meaning of things, such as language, music, painting, and physical gestures, has primacy and is located within the sensual, affective qualities of things themselves. "[T]he word has a meaning,"[21] and may as such be considered an embodied expression turned towards the world that actively seeks to open the tacit communication of things. In this perspective, the meaning of architecture is not located outside architecture itself; rather it comes into being through the experience of the physical materials of architecture itself.

Following Merleau-Ponty, Juhani Pallasmaa contends that this multisensory understanding of architecture is challenged by the domination of the visual sense. Arguing that contemporary architecture is sight-dominated and that the hegemony of vision has outdone the other senses, he criticises "ocularcentrism." To Pallasmaa, architecture should not address the senses separately but rather, quoting Merleau-Ponty, simultaneously through a multisensory approach: "My perception is [therefore] not a sum of visual, tactile and audible givens: I perceive in a total way with my whole being: I grasp a unique structure of the thing, a unique way of being, which speaks to all my senses at once."[22] According to Pallasmaa, the main problem in modern architecture is that we have lost the connection to the whole body, arguing that "[t]he current over-emphasis on the intellectual and conceptual dimensions of architecture contributes to the disappearance of its physical, sensual and embodied essence."[23]

Following the above, this chapter aims to contribute to the development of a more precise vocabulary for architectural design and phenomenological description. In continuation of Mies van der Rohe, it is argued that we must get a better understanding of materials and the way we articulate material qualities to enhance the quality of our physical environment. It is asked how we may articulate material qualities and experienced effects in a more nuanced manner – through a material (physical) vocabulary as well as a spoken (verbal) vocabulary. Offering an extensive vocabulary describing embodied communication, the so-called new phenomenology as developed by Hermann Schmitz is used as a lens and, in continuation, a verbal vocabulary capable of describing experienced material effects is proposed. Furthermore, an operational framework that may support articulating and operationalising experienced architectural phenomena is outlined. The aim is to get a better understanding of the matter of architecture based on lived experience specifically – and to be able to improve articulated architectural language in general.

Workshop

A work of architecture may be understood as a complex whole formed by a number of physical elements defined by shape, colour, proportion, material effects, etc., as suggested by Martin, Rasmussen, Petersen, and Zumthor as described above. In continuation, this chapter understands the physical material of architecture as a vocabulary in its own right that constitutes an architectural body taking part in embodied communication. As such, the physical properties and material qualities are considered inseparably connected to the experienced effects of architecture.

Aiming at sharpening both the material and verbal vocabulary for architectural design and description, two workshops were conducted with students from KTR. Taking an interest in how working with the physical material of architecture as a starting point may inform architectural design rather than the opposite, the workshops investigated selected aspects of the architectural whole. The investigations into the material effects of concrete[24] were motivated by the individual studies of the two semester assignments: the transformation of the former B&W and S&E buildings, respectively.[25] As part of the semester project, the workshops served the double purpose of physically working with and reflecting on the material as well as providing grounds for further analysis and valuation. The produced material samples in scale 1:1, representing materials in the two existing buildings, as well as material experiments for interventions into said buildings, were studied as individual elements in a studio setting with the aim of sharpening the general material language of the design projects, as well as forming a basis for developing a specific architectural vocabulary, as outlined above.

In the first workshop (W1), students were asked to produce two concrete samples, each of which reflected a material aspect of one of the existing buildings and, in addition, a transformation of or addition to the said sample. In the second workshop (W2), students were asked to produce a material composition according to the notions of "blend," "dialogue," or "contrast," coupling the concrete casts to reflect a material aspect of one of the existing buildings with a complementary material. The students were asked to describe the individual casts using the theoretical parameters for the appearance of ceramic glaze, defined by the ceramicist Linnet.[26] As such, the results of the workshop consisted of two parts: a number of concrete casts and an associated number of descriptions of technical material properties and experiential material qualities.

First, all the casts were documented, and the names assigned by the students were translated into English and entered on a data sheet, making comparison possible. The description of the technical properties and the material qualities, i.e. information on the material composition of the casts and the associated students' descriptions, were collected and studied in their totality and subsequently organised for analysis in Excel. The samples were finally documented photographically in a controlled setting.[27]

Second, 12 casts were selected to demonstrate different aspects of the casts, i.e. the shape of the mould, the surface of the formwork, and the composition of the cast. The selection was first ordered in pairs, each pair having one or two parameters in common. For instance, two casts – made with the same shape of the mould and the same surface of the formwork but with different pigments on the composition of the concrete – were paired.

Third, 12 casts that gave an embodied impulse of affective involvement were selected for further analysis. The final selection was made in accordance with the concept of embodied communication, as described by Schmitz,[28] and the experienced effects of the selected photographed casts were described by the authors. The final description thus comprises three levels: a complete description in accordance with the parameters as defined by Linnet; additional noteworthy observations; and finally, the experienced effects inspired by the concept of embodied communication as described by Schmitz.[29]

Finally, the students' descriptions and the description of the experienced effects were compared and analysed. The findings relating to A (the results of the workshop), B (the material effects), and C (the assigned descriptions) were discussed, and a conclusion was made. The photographs of the concrete casts produced in W1 and the descriptions of the individual casts from W1 are considered the data for the following analysis and are used as a basis in the subsequent discussion.

Material qualities and experienced effects

As materials play a key part in both the construction and experience of architecture, this chapter understands materials in a tripartite classification as property, quality, and effect. According to Hegger,

Drexler, and Zeumer, material meaning may be described as having three levels: a "visible" level, denoting the perceivable surface of a material as experienced by the senses; an "inner" level, as in the technical, mechanical, and chemical properties of a material; and an "associative" level, relating to memory.[30] Correspondingly, this chapter distinguishes between three levels of material meaning: a technical, mechanical, and chemical level of "material properties"; a visible level of "material qualities" as described by Linnet[31]; and a level of "experienced effects" as synaesthetic characters and suggestions of motion as described by Schmitz.[32]

Material qualities

Linnet's theoretical parameters for the visual appearance of ceramic glaze provide the (initial) systematic framework for the evaluation of material qualities[33]:

Nuance: violet/blue/green/yellow/orange/red/brown/grey/black/white
Purity: spectrally pure/luminous/muted/turbid/greyish
Lightness: light/medium/dark
Consistency: unicoloured/flecked/mottled (alt. speckled)/blotchy
Mattness: glossy (alt. shiny, bright, lustrous)/semi-glossy/satin matt/ matt/rough
Transparency: clear/transparent/opaque/lightproof
Thickness: layer of dust/thin/normal/thick/fat
Surface: smooth/coarse/boiled/cratered/crackled/crystals/branch shape/running
Texture: polished/glistering/gel-like/plaster-like/lint-like/metallic

Linnet points out that ceramic glaze can quite easily yield a different result than specified by a recipe, and he describes a number of material properties that influence the outcome, such as the purity of the raw materials, the effects of the biscuit or colour decorations, the thickness of the glaze, and the iron content of underpaint. He notes that in practice, we must learn from the specific glaze and about the specific nature of colour through systematic experimentation and testing in order to achieve the desired result. As described above, the students were asked to describe the casts made in the workshop using Linnet's theoretical parameters for the appearance of ceramic glaze. The material qualities defined by Linnet describe the wide range of visual appearances of ceramic glaze and provide an (initial) systematic framework for evaluating surfaces in general. However, Linnet does not address the experienced effects of the materials, let alone the experience of a work of architecture.

Experienced effects

From the perspective of so-called new phenomenology, Schmitz places the body as the basis of human experience, distinguishing the "material body" from the "felt body."[34] The material body is what we can examine objectively, whereas the felt body is the location of affective involvement manifested in corporeal impulses, which only the individual can experience. The often nonspecific, diffusely local-ised corporeal feelings oscillate between expansion and contraction in a pulsating rhythm without drawing on the material body or the five senses. Besides contraction and expansion, embodied dynamism is characterised by tension, swelling, intensity, rhythm, the proto-pathic and epicritic tendencies,[35] as well as embodied directionality. To illustrate the difference between protopathic and epicritic, Schmitz describes the former as the slow, strained, bulging, arched, unify-ing, dark, tough, and deep music of Beethoven and the latter as the pointed, powerful, tense, loose, dense, light, energetic, and fast-paced music of Mozart. The corporeal feelings are impulses such as fear and pain, emotions such as happiness and sadness, perceptual movements such as breathing in and out, and perceptual directions such as the extension of the gaze. The mediation between contraction and expan-sion is the basis of embodied communication that takes place when a body is absorbed by a corporeal dynamic which divides or connects it with the surroundings, such as a human body or a material body of architecture.[36]

This pre-linguistic communication is taking place through motion in itself or suggestions of motion in objects (whether static or moving) and through synaesthetic characters, i.e. intermodal properties of specific sensory qualities. Suggestions of motion are move-ments that are not being fully enacted which move the felt body in a certain direction through the expressiveness of an attitude, movement, gesture, gaze, or voice, such as the radiant, immer-sive, progressive, rotating, unfolding, contracting or swallowing, swelling, lifting, spreading, soaring through fatigue, lust, pride, and joy.[37] Resonant with Petersen's description of material effects, synaesthetic characters are form, texture, or colour characters that tune the body with qualitative expressions, such as the sharp, cutting, delicate, pointed, bright, hard, soft, warm, cold, heavy, massive, gentle, dense, smooth, roughness of colours, sounds, smells, sharpness, the bouncing or dragging gait, joy, enthusiasm, melancholy, freshness, and tiredness.[38] According to Schmitz, the body is a resonating antenna spreading and absorbing emotions as atmospheres.[39] To Schmitz, atmospheres may be defined as the "[...] unbounded occupation of a surfaceless space in the region of what is experienced as present."[40] An atmosphere is a mood that grips the felt body and transforms into emotions such as relaxed or tense. Emotions as atmospheres are experienced either as pure sensation of the atmospheres or as affective involvement. By means of suggestions of motion and synaesthetic characters, corporeal feelings as atmospheres are strengthened or lowered through pure sensation or affective involvement. As a result, embodied communication makes situations, defined by being whole, meaningful, and complex.[41]

Experienced effects may thus be understood as embodied communication taking place between the perceiver and the perceived. In this particular case, what is perceived is not the complex whole of architecture, but rather individual material elements holding specific qualities that, in continuation of Linnet, may be described in categories such as nuance, purity, and lightness. The way in which these material qualities are experienced may subsequently be described as synaesthetic characters and/or suggestions of motion that are strengthening or lowering corporeal feelings as atmospheres through pure sensation or affective involvement which, in continuation of Schmitz, may be described as sharp, blunt, hard, etc.

Inspired by Schmitz' concept of atmosphere, Gernot Böhme calls for a new aesthetic understanding of art and architecture.[42] To Böhme, aesthetics is about atmospheres and the well-being of people and is defined by three aspects: First, so-called "old" aesthetics is based on judgement and has less to do with sensuous experience. Second, language and semiotics have become dominating, overlooking the fact that a work of art has its own reality. Third, aesthetics is the full range of aesthetic work, understood as the production of atmospheres. To Böhme, aesthetics must be understood as something at work in the production as well as the perception of the work of art, a general theory of sensory experience. Criticising Schmitz' understanding of atmospheres as free floating, Böhme argues in favour of atmospheres as "something emanating from and produced by things, people, or their constellation."[43] However, with his focus on communication between bodies – whether static or in motion – Schmitz most radically transcends the division between subject and object in favour of the experienced effect through embodied interaction.

Models

Material vocabulary

The workshop (W1) resulted in 106 casts, all of high technical standard, with great variety in material qualities and many with material
effects of a high experiential quality (Figures 5.1–5.6). Even though all
the casts were made of the same material (concrete), primarily using

Figure 5.1 W1, concrete sample.

Figure 5.2 W1, concrete sample.

the same components (sand, cement, and supplementary materials), the experiential material qualities resulted in great variation. Many casts seem to be made with an intention to "experiment" as much as possible, in favour of the more systematic approach, for instance, by changing only one parameter at a time as suggested by Linnet. A preference for white portland cement is observed in the data as well as a preference for "strong" experiential effects, such as "expressive"

Figure 5.3 W1, pair 1 and 2.

forms, "heavy" relief, and "strong" colour in favour of more subtle experiential effects, such as colour nuance.

From an educational point of view, the enthusiasm manifested by the students may be considered a positive outcome of the workshop, as it allowed the students to experience the wide range of architectural possibilities inherent in a single material. Correspondingly, the high quality of technical properties, material qualities, and

Figure 5.4 W1, pair 3 and 6.

experiential effects of the casts themselves suggest a high degree of tacit knowledge and an ability to work with materials as a vocabulary in itself. This can be seen as a quality in its own right, making it visible to students (and others) that concrete is not just concrete, but a material with enormous potential for differentiation and architectural nuance.

Figure 5.5 W1, pair 3 and 6.

Technical properties and material qualities

With regard to the material investigation through "physical" concrete casts, the experiment may be described as successful. However, the students' "verbal" descriptions seemed to lack nuance and precision compared to the rich, nuanced experiential qualities of the casts themselves and the final description of experienced effects. In

Figure 5.6 W1, concrete samples.

many student descriptions, only a single word is used rather than a combination of words. There is a big difference in the word classes used, and the words often seem general in nature. For instance, words such as "tactile," "textural," and "haptic" do not describe the material quality specifically but reflect a general concept instead. Other words such as "massive" or "fragmented" describe the material qualities, whereas words like "gloomy," "volcanic," or "porcelain-like" are more associative. Architects and students of architecture, accustomed to practising tacit knowledge developed through designing architecture, may find it difficult to articulate what they are doing.

The categories suggested by Linnet[44] seem useful, but only to a certain extent. First, only a few of the categories were used. Second, some categories such as "thickness" or "texture" seem difficult to apply, possibly stemming from the fact that they relate to ceramic glaze. In addition, some categories seem to be missing, such as a more nuanced way of describing "lightness," "mattness," "play of shadows," "shape," and "colours in detail." The data regarding the description of the casts indicate that more attention should be given to distinguishing between the levels of material meaning, i.e. the technical, mechanical, and chemical levels of "material properties," the visible level of "material qualities," and the level of "experienced effects" as synaesthetic characters.

Experienced effects

The data suggest that a phenomenological description using synaesthetic characters – including sharp, cutting, delicate, pointy, bright, hard, soft, warm, cold, heavy, massive, gentle, dense, smooth, and rough – has great potential. The list of synaesthetic characters may be widened to include words such as dry, nervous, delicate, gentle, bare, and vibrant. They also suggest that the rich, nuanced experience of material effects – even if isolated from an even richer and more nuanced, complex whole – defies simple description but must be further developed and complemented.

All in all, the concrete casts themselves articulate a rich, precise "material" vocabulary in their own right, thus constituting a successful part of the experiment, whereas the "verbal" articulation of the visible level of "material qualities" did not meet the same level of nuance and precision. The results indicate that architects and students of architecture (at master's level) have a well-developed material vocabulary and that spoken architectural language should be further developed.

Vocabulary

Workshop

Architecture is a complex, multifaceted discipline synthesising technical, functional, and aesthetic parameters as described by Vitruvius more than two thousand years ago.[45] The question is does it make any sense to break down the experience of architecture into smaller elements as, in this case, concrete samples of A4 dimensions? If, as argued above, architecture is a rich, embodied communication between the perceiver and the perceived, there may be a risk of reducing the quality of the experience to a simplified, objective question. Analysing an individual architectural element may be criticised as an attempt to put the complexity of architectural experience into a formula. Similarly, if the experience of architecture is characterised by feelings as atmospheres, the fullness of the experience is reduced when each element is analysed separately. The embodied experience of each individual element is undoubtedly reduced when taken out of its specific "context." Parameters such as the size of the individual element, relation to other materials, position in space, and light conditions are left out of the experiment. For instance, a cast may be experienced quite differently when placed next to one material as opposed to another. Similarly, the controlled setting in the documentation process allows the individual casts to be compared individually, however, not in changing light conditions as would be the case in the completed work. Furthermore, the documentation photographs taken in the controlled setting leave out questions concerning physical "interaction." The experience of a material experienced from far away in a larger setting is quite different from experiencing the same material from a moderate distance, which in turn is quite different from experiencing the material close up. Finally, the experiment leaves out the question of "time." For instance, the weathering effects of rain, sun, and changing temperatures, and the question of deterioration and decay are left out of the experiment.

Isolating individual elements reduces the rich, nuanced experience and, in so doing, may be described as problematic. On the other hand, when architecture can be understood as embodied communication, as suggested by Schmitz, the quality of the communication is necessarily dependent on the composition of the individual elements, just as it is dependent on the receptiveness of the perceiver. To Schmitz, the dwelling [*die Wohnung*] is where emotions are cultivated in the enclosed [*umfriedeten*] space, giving humans the opportunity to create the right mood and provide an intense and nuanced emotional climate.[46] As such, architectural space may be understood as a synthesis of parts comprising physical elements that may be viewed independently to create a whole, meaningful, and complex situation. The workshop analysis is concerned with the individual parts, in this case the material properties, material qualities, and experiential effects of the concrete casts, well knowing that the experience of architecture is a rich, nuanced totality.

Framework

The high quality of the produced casts points to the rich potential of exploring material qualities as a fundamental part of architectural design. The casts themselves may be understood as a kind of "material vocabulary" which, in continuation of Schmitz, may evoke feelings as atmospheres through pure sensation or affective involvement, moving the felt body in a specific way. In the Arts, physical material may in fact be understood as a vocabulary in its own right, communicating an emotional content. Agnes Martin's carefully pencilled grids on square canvases washed with pale colours, which make present a gentle play of textural effects and vibrating sensations of lines that puts the perceiver in a specific emotional state. To Martin "[a]rt is the concrete representation of our most subtle feelings."[47] Constituting a distinctive material vocabulary when the physical material is perceived, "[w]e do not just look, we make a definite response to the work. As we look at it, we are happier or sadder, more at peace or more depressed. A work may stimulate yearning, helplessness, belligerence, or remorse."[48] In the perspective of archaeology, Bjørnar Olsen points out, "[...] things are not words nor are they primary signs to be read or products ready to be consumed or 'sublated'. Things possess their own nonverbal qualities and are involved in their own material and historical process that cannot be disclosed unless we explore their integrity qua things."[49] In this perspective, the concrete casts themselves may be considered a material language in their own right, which may be nuanced and specified through material properties. Similarly, a verbal vocabulary – defined by the combination of material qualities and experienced effects, as based on the framework by Linnet in conjunction with the synaesthetic characters by Schmitz – may hold great potential that calls for further development, including, for instance, parameters such as context, interaction, and time, as described above.

Vocabulary

Architecture may be described in multiple ways. The art historian may describe a building as a trace of a particular societal development manifested in the form of styles; the sociologist may consider a house a spatial expression of human negotiation; and the engineer may perceive a structure as the result of a technological necessity. Undoubtedly, style categories, sign theory, and semiotic analysis make it possible to systematise and categorise formal characteristics

and make it easier to describe and communicate architectural properties. However, criticising the restricted mode of natural science,
phenomenology opposes the aim for objectivity, conceptualisation,
and categorisation. Arguing that "[...] we must go back to the 'things
themselves',"[50] Edmund Husserl directs focus on the world as it presents itself to consciousness in its intuitive givenness, as opposed to
the dominant empiric reductionism. Returning to the perceptual
world, the phenomenological first-person perspective challenges
the dogmatic division of the world into subject and object as aimed
for by the disembodied perspective of natural science. Arguing that
Western philosophical tradition has destroyed the dynamic of the
body and divided humans into body and soul,[51] Schmitz similarly
transcends this division in favour of understanding the human relationship to the physical environment as a question of embodied
communication.

Understanding architecture in merely objective terms may be considered a confirmation of the dogmatic division of the world into
subject and object, resulting in a reinforced subject-object dualism
that may emphasise an idea of the world in general and architecture
specifically as objectively mechanical. It may, however, be argued
that the material vitality of the world in fact "is me, it predates me,
it exceeds me, it postdates me,"[52] as Jane Bennett argues from the
perspective of political science. Ultimately, reducing the vibrant
matter of architecture to merely inert building stuff may risk producing buildings that do not support a sensitive, embodied being in the
world, leading to a further distancing from the physical body as well
as from the natural world. Aiming at a specific vocabulary for architectural description, objectivity, conceptualisation, and categorisation should not be put entirely aside. Rather, a vocabulary in closer
relation to the body of the perceiver as well as the body of architecture might "encourage more intelligent and sustainable engage-
ments with vibrant matter"[53] and be a critical addition to an already
existing language that might better support the "cultivation of the
emotions" through a verbal and material architectural vocabulary.

Perspectives

If it is correct that physical materials formed as building elements
in themselves form a material vocabulary specified through specific
material properties and that a vocabulary of material qualities and
experienced effects has the potential to describe and develop architectural design, this may be consequential for how we teach, design, and

communicate architecture. In teaching, focus should be intensified on producing material elements as a way for the student to develop a material architectural language. In addition, the verbal vocabulary based on embodied communication should be developed as a way to discuss and advance the material vocabulary more systematically. In teaching and designing architecture, a more systematic approach to the relationship between material qualities and experienced effects could also be fruitful when aimed at designing buildings with more eloquent architectural qualities. Similarly, a more systematic approach in the design process might help communicate the architectural design to others, clients, contractors, and authorities alike. This could be relevant when designing new buildings and when working with existing buildings but could also be relevant when conducting surveys, in the sketching process, and in the project phase.

Criticising the domination of vision, Pallasmaa argues, "[a]s buildings lose their plasticity, and their connection with the language and wisdom of the body, they become isolated in the cool and distant realm of vision."[54] Today, designing architecture may be criticised as mere image-making, focused on creating pictures that should only be experienced from a distance without engaging the other senses or the felt body. According to Pallasmaa, "vision separates us from the world, whereas the other senses unite us with the world."[55] If this is true, then perhaps intensifying focus on physical, material quality and embodied experienced effects in architecture could help humans connect more profoundly to the world. Just as Schmitz understands the body as a "resonating antenna" communicating with other bodies, Bennett believes in "one matter-energy, the maker of things seen and unseen."[56] Aiming to "detach materiality from the figures of passive, mechanistic, or divinely infused substance,"[57] Bennett understands physical matter as "doing things," arguing that "encounters with lively matter can chasten my fantasies of human mastery, highlight the common materiality of all that is, expose a wider distribution of agency, and reshape the self and its interests."[58] In this perspective, physical building elements can be understood as a material language which is one way for human beings to communicate with the common world.

Conclusion

As Polanyi asserted, tacit knowledge may be difficult to articulate verbally, and it seems that words have a tendency to slip and slide when working with aesthetics. Describing how magenta, for example, is now considered pink but originally thought of as purple-red, Kassia St Clair points at the discrepancies between the name a society gives a colour and the actual colour, and how these may shift over time.[59] As Rasmussen points out, "[w]ords can put you on the right track but you have to experience the textural effects yourself to realise what it is all about."[60] The question is how can we articulate material qualities and experienced effects in a more nuanced manner – physically as well as verbally – as motivated by material investigations and descriptions produced in two workshops? As described above, the workshops resulted in a large number of casts, all of high technical standard with a wide variety of material qualities and many with material effects of an exceptional experiential quality. It is quite clear that concrete is not just concrete but holds great potential for nuancing and emphasising architectural vocabulary when designing, teaching, and communicating architecture. Although the knowledge produced in the workshop to a certain degree remained tacit, the individual casts had an ability to enter into meaningful situations – when thinking "with" the material rather than thinking "of" the material. As such, the wide variety of colour, textural effects, relief, etc. offers a wide range of expressions that may be articulated and experienced through embodied communication. In this perspective, material qualities and effects may be understood as part of a nuanced architectural vocabulary in their own right. The quality of the material parameters – such as nuance, purity, lightness, consistency, mattness, transparency, thickness, surface, and texture – affects the felt body as embodied communication through corporeal feelings. As synaesthetic characters, the material qualities move or tune the felt body with qualitative effects that strengthen or lower the corporeal feelings as atmospheres, making meaningful situations.

If architecture constitutes a rich, nuanced language in its own right, the limitation of a verbal architectural language is that it will always be insufficient. While material architectural language may be understood as an embodied presentation of the content itself, verbal architectural language will always remain a subordinate description of a phenomenon seen "from the outside." In return, the potential of a verbal language – founded on an embodied architectural language – is that fixed categories, formalistic rules, and preconceived judgement may be avoided. Rather than being restricted to the categories of semiotics, signs, and symbols, spoken material language may articulate embodied material effects such as the sharp, cutting, delicate, pointy, bright, hard, soft, warm, cold, heavy, massive, gentle, dense, smooth, rough, dry, nervous, delicate, gentle, bare, and vibrant. As such, a vivid architectural language may evolve, allowing for a description of not what architecture looks like, but rather what it does.

In an educational setting, this means that teaching architecture is not simply a neutral impartation of knowledge from one person with insight to another without. Embodied knowledge is not quantifiable as if being filled into an empty vessel. In contrast, focusing on experienced material effects rather than formal categories could enable teaching to be a dynamic process in which both teacher and student are affected and transformed. Describing what architecture actually does rather than how architecture looks, the education of architects could be founded on mutual formation instead of encyclopaedic trivia or theoretical exercises. In this perspective, articulating the experienced material effects could contribute to a rich, nuanced architectural practice that is not misled by spectacular concepts and superfluous effects. Instead, a verbal language rooted in embodied communication through synaesthetic characters and suggestions of motion could engage in the dynamic development and communication of profound architectural wisdom.

Based on this, it is proposed that the outlined framework – defined as an interrelation of material properties, qualities, and experienced effects – could constitute the basis of a more systematic, comprehensive, and nuanced vocabulary which could support better architectural education and design-practice and encourage a more precise articulation and communication of intentions. As a verbal language based on embodied communication with physical material, a more precise vocabulary has the potential to develop a rich, nuanced architectural culture as part of the "common materiality" of all that is.

Just as making is not enough, talking is not enough, either. Instead, the dynamic interrelation of a physical material language and an embodied verbal language could be a way to strengthen both. As such, speaking and making are not deemed two separate paths comprising an isolated verbal and an isolated material vocabulary. Describing how meaning and matter are closely interconnected to the skilled practitioner, Schmitz points out, "[...] the poet, from the states of affairs, programs and problems, in elegant austerity weaves a net so thin that the situational network invoked by him, especially in extended and complex lyrics, transpires in its entirety."[61] Similarly, the verbal and material vocabularies in architecture are interrelated as variations of one another in the coming to presentation of the language of architecture through spoken matter.

Notes

1 Wiel Arets et al., eds., "Ludwig Mies van der Rohe, Inaugural Address as Director of Architecture at IIT, 20 November 1938," in *Nowness 2013 2014 IIT Architecture Chicago* (Chicago: IITAC Press, 2014), 14.
2 Ibid. 14.
3 Ibid. 15.
4 Beatriz Colomina and Mark Wigley, *Are We Human?* (Zürich: Lars Müller Publishers, 2016), 96.
5 Juhani Pallasmaa, *The Eyes of the Skin* (Chichester: John Wiley & Sons, 2005), 15–32.
6 David Leatherbarrow, *Architecture Oriented Otherwise* (New York: Princeton Architectural Press, 2009), 26.
7 Kasha Linville, "Agnes Martin: An Appreciation." *Artforum 9* (1971), 72.
8 Ibid. 73.
9 Peter Zumthor, *Thinking Architecture* (Basel, Birkhäuser, 2010), 20.
10 Ibid. 20.
11 Michael Polanyi, *The Tacit Dimension* (New York: Anchor Books, Doubleday, 1967), 4.
12 Donald Schön, *The Reflective Practitioner* (Århus: Klim, 2001).
13 Nicolai B. Andersen, "Phenomenological Method," in *Formation – Architectural Education in a Nordic Perspective,* edited by E. Lorentsen et al. (Copenhagen: Architectural Publisher B, 2018), 74–95.
14 Carl Petersen, *Stoflige Virkninger* (Copenhagen: Arkitekten, 1919).
15 Steen E. Rasmussen, *Experiencing Architecture* (Cambridge: MIT Press, 1959), 18.
16 Ibid. 32.
17 Ibid. 32.
18 Maurice Merleau-Ponty, *Phenomenology of Perception* (London: Routledge, 1962), 25.
19 Komarine Romdenh-Romluc, *Merleau-Ponty and Phenomenology of Perception* (London: Routledge, 2011), 187.
20 Merleau-Ponty, *Phenomenology of Perception*, 209.
21 Ibid. 206.
22 Pallasmaa, *The Eyes of the Skin*, 21.
23 Ibid. 32.
24 The climate crises call for strong and sustained reductions in emissions of carbon dioxide and other greenhouse gases as stated ever more convincingly by the IPCC, Sixth Assessment Report 2021. The use of concrete – being a major contributor to the GHG emissions – should therefore be significantly reduced in the future.
25 Burmeister & Wain administrative headquarters, Suenson, 1962. Schou-Epa building, KKET, 1970.
26 Erik Linnet, *Keramiker Nøglen* (Gylling: Narayana Press, 2017), 40.
27 The photographic setting consisted of a neutral-grey card ground plane with a white painted wall as backplane. As a fully contained lighting set-up was unavailable, a combination of diffuse daylight and strobes was used. The set-up was arranged as a flat triangle with the casts at the peak, a 400-watt strobe (set to ≈ 300 watts) equipped with a Ø120-cm soft box combined with diffuse daylight to the left and a 400-watt strobe

(set to ≈ 150 watts) equipped with a Ø60-cm soft box to the right. The lighting set-up provided a consistent illumination of the casts and yielded minor variations in the context illumination. The digital camera (Sony A7II + Sony FE 55mm F1.8 ZA) was continuously calibrated for light temperature using a Datacolor SpyderCheckr 24 card. Photographs were subsequently processed in Adobe Lightroom for a comparative result.

28 Hermann Schmitz, *New Phenomenology* (Milan: Mimesis International, 2019).
29 Ibid.
30 Manfred Hegger; M., Hans Drexler and Martin Zeumer, *Basics – Materials* (Basel: Birkhäuser, 2006), 8.
31 Linnet, *Keramiker Nøglen*, 40.
32 Schmitz, *New Phenomenology*, 68. Hermann Schmitz, *Kort indføring i den nye fænomenologi* (Aalborg: Aalborg Universitetsforlag, 2017), 30–31. Hermann Schmitz, *Kroppen* (Aalborg: Aalborg Universitetsforlag, 2017), 39.
33 Linnet, *Keramiker Nøglen*, 40.
34 Schmitz, *New Phenomenology*.
35 Schmitz, *Kroppen*, 66 ff.
36 Ibid. 35 ff.
37 Ibid. 40
38 Ibid. 43.
39 Ibid. 122.
40 Schmitz, *New Phenomenology*, 94.
41 Schmitz, *Kort indføring i den nye fænomenologi*, 35–36.
42 Gernot Böhme, *Atmospheric Architectures* (London: Bloomsbury, 2017), 14–17.
43 Ibid. 23.
44 Linnet, *Keramiker Nøglen*, 40.
45 Vitruvius, *The Ten Books on Architecture* (Cambridge: Harvard University Press, 1914), 17.
46 Hermann Schmitz, *Der Leib, der Raum und die Gefühle* (Bielefeld: Aisthesis Verlag, 2015), 46ff.
47 As cited in Kathryn Tuma, "Enhancing Stillness: The Art of Agnes Martin," in *3 X Abstraction: New Methods of Drawing*, edited by Catherine de Zegher et al. (New Haven: Yale University Press, 2005), 50.
48 Ibid. 42.
49 Bjørnar Olsen, *In Defence of Things* (California: Alta Mira, 2010), 172.
50 Edmund Husserl, *Logical Investigations* (London: Routledge, 2001), 168.
51 Schmitz, *Kroppen*, 81.
52 Jane Bennett, *Vibrant Matter* (Durham: Duke University Press, 2009), 120.
53 Ibid. viii.
54 Pallasmaa, *The Eyes of the Skin*, 31.
55 Ibid. 25.
56 Bennett, *Vibrant Matter*, 122.
57 Ibid. xiii.
58 Ibid. 122.
59 Kassia St Clair, *The Secret Lives of Colour* (London: John Murray, 2016), 26.

60 Rasmussen, *Experiencing Architecture*, 164.
61 Schmitz, *New Phenomenology*, 78.

Bibliography

Andersen, Nicolai B. "Phenomenological Method." In *Formation – Architectural Education in a Nordic Perspective*, edited by E. Lorentsen and K.A. Torp. Copenhagen: Architectural Publisher B, 2018.
Arets, Wiel et al. "Ludwig Mies van der Rohe, Inaugural Address as Director of Architecture at IIT, 20 November 1938." In *Nowness 2013 2014 IIT Architecture Chicago*. Chicago, IL: IITAC Press, 2014.
Bennett, Jane. *Vibrant Matter: A Political Ecology of Things*. Durham, NC: Duke University Press, 2009.
Böhme, Gernot. *Atmospheric Architectures: The Aesthetics of Felt Spaces*. London: Bloomsbury, 2017.
Colomina, Beatriz and Wigley, Mark. *Are We Human? Notes on Archaeology of Design*. Zürich: Lars Müller Publishers, 2016.
Ellen MacArthur Foundation. *What Is Circular Economy?* Accessed 21 August 2021, https://www.ellenmacarthurfoundation.org/circular-economy/concept.
Hegger, Manfred, Drexler, Hans and Zeumer, Martin. *Basics – Materials*. Basel: Birkhäuser, 2006.
Husserl, Edmund. *Logical Investigations*. London: Routledge, 2001.
IPCC. "Summary for Policymakers." In *Climate Change 2021: The Physical Science Basis*. Cambridge: Cambridge University Press, 2021.
Leatherbarrow, David. *Architecture Oriented Otherwise*. New York, NY: Princeton Architectural Press, 2009.
Linnet, Erik. *Keramiker Nøglen*. Gylling: Narayana Press, 2017.
Linville, Kasha. "Agnes Martin: An Appreciation." *Artforum* 9 (1971), pp. 72–73.
Merleau-Ponty, Maurice. *Phenomenology of Perception*. London: Routledge, 1962.
Olsen, Bjørnar. *In Defence of Things: Archaeology and the Ontology of Objects*. California: Alta Mira, 2010.
Pallasmaa, Juhani. *The Eyes of the Skin*. Chichester: John Wiley & Sons, 2005.
Petersen, Carl. "Textures." In *Nordisk Klassicism, Nordic Classicism 1910–1930*, edited by S. Paavilainen. Helsinki: Museum of Finnish Architecture, 1982.
Polanyi, Michael. *The Tacit Dimension*. New York, NY: Anchor Books, Doubleday, 1967.
Rasmussen, Steen E. *Experiencing Architecture*. Cambridge: MIT Press, 1959.
Romdenh-Romluc, Komarine. *Merleau-Ponty and Phenomenology of Perception*. London: Routledge, 2011.
Schmitz, Hermann. *Der Leib, der Raum und die Gefühle*. Bielefeld: Aisthesis Verlag, 2015.
Schmitz, Hermann. *Kort indføring i den nye fænomenologi*. Aalborg: Aalborg Universitetsforlag, 2017.

Schmitz, Hermann. *Kroppen*. Aalborg: Aalborg Universitetsforlag, 2017.

Schmitz, Hermann. *New Phenomenology. A Brief Introduction*. Milan: Mimesis International, 2019.

Schön, Donald. *The Reflective Practitioner: How Professionals Think in Action*. Århus: Klim, 2001.

St Clair, Kassia. *The Secret Lives of Colour*. London: John Murray, 2016.

Tuma, Kathryn. "Enhancing Stillness: The Art of Agnes Martin." In *3 X Abstraction: New Methods of Drawing*, edited by Catherine de Zegher and Hendel Teicher, 41–58. New Haven, CT: Yale University Press, 2005.

Vitruvius, Marcus. *The Ten Books on Architecture*. Cambridge: Harvard University Press, 1914.

Zumthor, Peter. *Thinking Architecture*. Basel: Birkhäuser, 2010.

Index

Note: *Italic* page numbers refer to figures; page numbers followed by 'n' refer to notes.

For Product Safety Concerns and Information please contact our EU
representative GPSR@taylorandfrancis.com Taylor & Francis Verlag GmbH,
Kaufingerstraße 24, 80331 München, Germany

Printed and bound by CPI Group (UK) Ltd, Croydon, CR0 4YY
11/04/2025
01844010-0013